THE AUTOBIOGRAPHY OF A CAD

by Ian Hislop & Nick Newman

adapted from the novel by
A.G. Macdonell

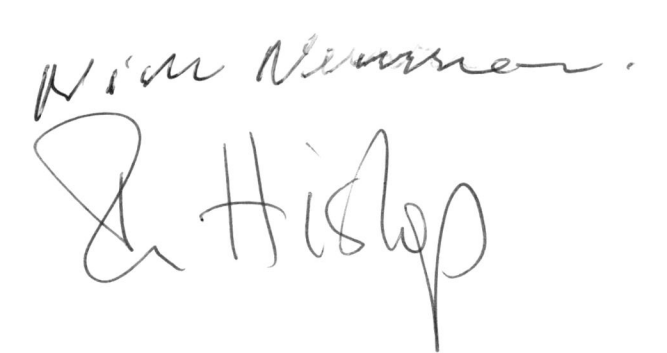

[signatures: Nick Newman, Ian Hislop]

SAMUEL FRENCH

Copyright © 2025 by Ian Hislop & Nick Newman
Cover artwork by Rebecca Pitt
All Rights Reserved

THE AUTOBIOGRAPHY OF A CAD is fully protected under the copyright laws of the British Commonwealth, including Canada, the United States of America, and all other countries of the Copyright Union. All rights, including professional and amateur stage productions, recitation, lecturing, public reading, motion picture, radio broadcasting, television, online/digital production, and the rights of translation into foreign languages are strictly reserved.

ISBN 978-0-573-00075-1

concordtheatricals.co.uk

concordtheatricals.com

FOR AMATEUR PRODUCTION ENQUIRIES

UNITED KINGDOM AND WORLD
EXCLUDING NORTH AMERICA
licensing@concordtheatricals.co.uk
020-7054-7298

Each title is subject to availability from Concord Theatricals, depending upon country of performance.

CAUTION: Professional and amateur producers are hereby warned that *THE AUTOBIOGRAPHY OF A CAD* is subject to a licensing fee. The purchase, renting, lending or use of this book does not constitute a licence to perform this title(s), which licence must be obtained from the appropriate agent prior to any performance. Performance of this title(s) without a licence is a violation of copyright law and may subject the producer and/or presenter of such performances to penalties. Both amateurs and professionals considering a production are strongly advised to apply to the appropriate agent before starting rehearsals, advertising, or booking a theatre. A licensing fee must be paid whether the title is presented for charity or gain and whether or not admission is charged.

This work is published by Samuel French, an imprint of Concord Theatricals Ltd.

The Professional Rights in this play are controlled by Casarotto Ramsay & Associates, Ltd., 3rd Floor, 7 Savoy Court, Strand, London, WC2R 0EX.

No one shall make any changes in this title for the purpose of production. No part of this book may be reproduced, stored in a retrieval system, scanned, uploaded, or transmitted in any form, by any means, now known or yet to be invented, including mechanical, electronic, digital, photocopying, recording, videotaping, or otherwise, without the prior written permission of the publisher. No one shall share this title, or part of this title, to any social media or file hosting websites.

The moral right of Ian Hislop & Nick Newman to be identified as author of this work has been asserted in accordance with Section 77 of the Copyright, Designs and Patents Act 1988.

USE OF COPYRIGHTED MUSIC

A licence issued by Concord Theatricals to perform this play does not include permission to use the incidental music specified in this publication. In the United Kingdom: Where the place of performance is already licensed by the PERFORMING RIGHT SOCIETY (PRS) a return of the music used must be made to them. If the place of performance is not so licensed then application should be made to PRS for Music (www.prsformusic.com). A separate and additional licence from PHONOGRAPHIC PERFORMANCE LTD (www.ppluk.com) may be needed whenever commercial recordings are used. Outside the United Kingdom: Please contact the appropriate music licensing authority in your territory for the rights to any incidental music.

USE OF COPYRIGHTED THIRD-PARTY MATERIALS

Licensees are solely responsible for obtaining formal written permission from copyright owners to use copyrighted third-party materials (e.g., artworks, logos) in the performance of this play and are strongly cautioned to do so. If no such permission is obtained by the licensee, then the licensee must use only original materials that the licensee owns and controls. Licensees are solely responsible and liable for clearances of all third-party copyrighted materials, and shall indemnify the copyright owners of the play(s) and their licensing agent, Concord Theatricals Ltd., against any costs, expenses, losses and liabilities arising from the use of such copyrighted third-party materials by licensees.

IMPORTANT BILLING AND CREDIT REQUIREMENTS

If you have obtained performance rights to this title, please refer to your licensing agreement for important billing and credit requirements.

NOTE

This edition reflects a rehearsal draft of the script and may differ from the final production.

THE AUTOBIOGRAPHY OF A CAD was first presented at the Watermill Theatre, Newbury, on 7 February 2025. It was based on the novel by A.G. Macdonell, adapted by Ian Hislop & Nick Newman. The cast and creative team were as follows:

EDWARD FOX-INGLEBY............................. James Mack
MISS CONSTANCE APPLEBY..................... Rhiannon Neads
MR HENRY COLLINS................................Mitesh Soni
Director ....Paul Hart
Set & Costume Design ....Ceci Calf
Lighting Design .... Charly Dunford
Sound Design ....Steven Atkinson
Projection Design................................. Rachel Sampley
Choreographer ....Emily Holt
Assistant Director .... Elsa Strachan
Assistant Set & Costume Design.......................... Jacob Wu
Assistant Lighting Design ....Nicola Crawford

The **Watermill Theatre** is a small but mighty 200-seat theatre, set in idyllic gardens and nestled on the banks of the river Lambourn in rural West Berkshire, southeast England.

The Watermill Theatre is a unique producing powerhouse of residential and artistic facilities which provide a crucible for creativity, innovative storytelling, and artistic excellence. The Watermill's mission is to make theatre that is surprising, inventive, and exciting and to enable access for everyone. A hallmark of its work is the artistry of actor-musicianship, in both new writing and reinvigorated classics. The theatre nurtures and celebrates talent and creativity in its company, community, and in the wider sector and it holds wellbeing, equity, and sustainability at the heart of its culture.

In 2024, the Watermill was awarded the prestigious title of 'Theatre of the Year' jointly with the National Theatre. This award, recognising excellence in British theatre, was bestowed on the Watermill Theatre for its continued ambition as an independent charity, and the success of their 2023 production of *The Lord of the Rings*. This multi award-winning production, the Watermill's most ambitious to date, has subsequently transferred to Chicago, Auckland, and Australia (tour) before it returns to the UK in October 2025.

Reaching far beyond the 200 seats in its auditorium, the Watermill's productions regularly transfer to the West End or tour the UK and internationally, including *Spike, Calamity Jane, Bleak Expectations, Crazy for You, The Wipers Times* and *Trial By Laughter*. *The Autobiography of a Cad* is the fifth production written by Ian Hislop and Nick Newman for the Watermill, following *A Bunch of Amateurs, The Wipers Times, Trial By Laughter* and *Spike*.

With a core belief in the transformative power of the arts, the Watermill Theatre also runs a comprehensive outreach programme, working with children and young people, those from low-income backgrounds, and isolated or displaced communities.

Artistic Director Paul Hart

Executive Director Claire Murray

watermill.org.uk

CAST

JAMES MACK | Cad/Edward Fox-Ingleby

Training: The Guildhall School of Music and Drama

Watermill credits include: *Much Ado About Nothing* (2024); *Spike* (2022); *The Hound of the Baskervilles* (2020); *The Rivals* (2018); *Macbeth* (2015) and *Journey's End* (2014).

Theatre credits include: *Spike* (UK Tour); *Burke & Hare* (New Wolsey Theatre); *Cinderella, One Man, Two Guvnors* (Torch Theatre); *Robin Hood* (The Old Market Theatre, Brighton); *Ragtime* (Charing Cross Theatre); *The Provok'd Wife* (Go People and Tour); *Dr. Faustus* (Matchstick Theatre Company); *Mermaid* (London Shuffle Festival); *This Heaven* (Finborough Theatre); *Hay Fever* (Duke of Yorks, West End); *A Christmas Carol* (Old Red Lion); *Julius Caesar* (Sam Wanamaker Festival, Shakespeare's Globe); *The Jailer's Tale* (ArtsDepot); *Confusions* and *The Insect Play* (Theatre Royal Haymarket).

TV and Film credits include: *Bad Snappers* (Comedy Central) and *Embryonic* (Door 77 Films).

RHIANNON NEADS | Miss Constance Appleby and others

Training: LAMDA

Theatre credits include: *Supernova* (Omnibus Theatre); *All Lies* (Alan Ayckbourn Company); *The Wind Of Heaven* (Finborough); *3 Billion Seconds* (Paines Plough Roundabout); *Leia and the Roman* (VAULT Festival); *Mary's Babies* (Oak Theatre) and *Great Expectations* (Merton Arts).

TV and Film credits include: *One Day* (Netflix); *Call The Midwife, Blitz with Lucy Worsley, Father Brown* and *Doctors* (BBC); *Wilding* (Amazon Prime) *and Downton Abbey* (ITV).

Audio credits include: *Lenin Forever, Harland, English Rose, Not With the Eyes, Sappho, The Blue Lenses, Vital Signs* and *Home Front* (all for BBC Radio). Rhiannon is the host of espionage podcast *True Spies* (Spyscape Studios).

Rhiannon is one half of musical comedy duo Stiff & Kitsch whose shows include: *Adele Is Younger Than Us* (Pleasance, Edinburgh) and *Bricking It* (Soho Theatre). Their work has been featured on BBC Three, Comedy Central and *The Now Show* (BBC Radio 4).

MITESH SONI | Mr Henry Collins and others

Training: Guildford School of Acting

Theatre credits include: *A Midsummer Night's Dream* (RSC and Barbican); *A Christmas Carol* (RSC); *The Play What I Wrote* (Birmingham Rep and UK Tour); *Oliver Twist* (Leeds Playhouse); *Jack & The Beanstalk* and *Cinderella* (Oldham Coliseum); *Twelfth Night, Henry V, The Borrowers, The Tempest, Much Ado About Nothing* and *Swallows & Amazons* (Chester, Storyhouse); *The Big Corner, East Is East* and *Hamlet* (Octagon, Bolton); *A Christmas Carol* (Hull Truck); *Combustion* (Arcola Theatre and Tara UK Tour); *Home Truths* (Bunker Theatre and Cardboard Citz); *Rudolf* (West Yorkshire Playhouse); *Coming Up* (Watford Palace); *Macbeth* (Tara Arts and UK Tour); *Romeo & Juliet* (National Theatre); *The Good Person of Sichuan* (Colchester); *Arabian Nights* (Manchester Library Theatre); *The Firework Maker's Daughter* (Theatre by the Lake, Keswick); *The Rise & Fall of Little Voice* (Dukes, Lancaster); *Peter Pan* (New Vic Stoke); *Rafta Rafta* (Octagon Bolton and New Vic Stoke); *The Jungle Book* (Birmingham Stage Company UK Tour); *Mercury Fur* (Goldsmiths); *Lord of the Flies* (Pilot Theatre UK tour) and *Meteorite* (Hampstead Theatre).

Film credits include: *A Christmas No. 1, Medusa Deluxe, Mughal Mowgli Rise of The Footsolider 2* and *Syriana*.

Television credits include: *Juice, EastEnders, Silent Witness, The Pact, The Agency* and *The Canterbury Tales* (BBC); *Hollyoaks* and *Run* (Channel 4); *Ted's Top Ten* (ITV) and *Threesome* (Comedy Central).

Awards: Asian Media Awards – Best Production (*Combustion*) and Manchester Theatre Award – Best Ensemble (*Arabian Nights*).

CREATIVE

IAN HISLOP | Writer

Ian Hislop is a writer, journalist and broadcaster. He was educated at Ardingly College and Magdalen College, Oxford. He has been editor of *Private Eye* since 1986. He has been a regular team captain on the BBC show *Have I Got News for You* since 1990. In 2018, Ian curated an exhibition at the British Museum, *I Object: Ian Hislop's Search for Dissent*. He has appeared on *BBC Question Time*, written and presented documentaries for television and radio about various subjects including the Patron Saints of the British Isles, History of Tax, Female Hymn Writers, Dr Beeching, Victorian Philanthropists, Benefit Systems, the First World War, and The Stiff Upper Lip. In 2024, he had two series on Radio 4: *Ian Hislop's Oldest Jokes* and *Orwell vs Kafka*, with Helen Lewis. In 2024, Ian was presented with a Fellowship Award by the Society of Editors.

As a scriptwriter with Nick Newman, his work includes five years on *Spitting Image*, *Harry Enfield and Chums*, and *My Dad's the Prime Minister* as well as numerous radio series. They have had four plays premiered at The Watermill – *A Bunch of Amateurs*, *The Wipers Times*, *Trial by Laughter*, and *Spike*. These subsequently went on to further success including national tours, West End transfers and critical acclaim.

NICK NEWMAN | Writer

Nick Newman is an award-winning cartoonist and writer. He has worked for *Private Eye* since 1981 and has been pocket cartoonist for *The Sunday Times* since 1989. His cartoons have appeared in many other publications including *The Guardian*, *Punch* and *The Spectator*. He was The Cartoon Art Trust's Gag Cartoonist of the Year in 1997, 1998, 2005 and 2016. In 2013 he edited the humour bestseller *Private Eye: A Cartoon History*.

His collaboration with Ian Hislop began with *Spitting Image*, and continued with Dawn French's *Murder Most Horrid* and *The Harry Enfield Show* – with the creation of Tim Nice-But-Dim. They also wrote the BBC1 film *Gobble* and the sitcom *My Dad's the Prime Minister*. In 2008 their film *A Bunch of Amateurs* was chosen for the Royal Film Performance. Their BBC film *The Wipers Times* won the Broadcast Press Guild Award for best single drama, and was nominated for a BAFTA, before its stage adaptation. Radio credits include many series of *Dave Podmore* for Radio 4, along with *Mastering the Universe*, starring Dawn French. With Ian Hislop, he also wrote Radio 4's *Gush*, *Greed All About It*, *The News at Bedtime* and *Trial by Laughter*. *The Autobiography of a Cad* is the duo's fifth collaboration with the Watermill Theatre.

PAUL HART | Director

Paul is the current Artistic Director and Joint CEO of Watermill Theatre.

Watermill credits include: *Much Ado About Nothing* (2024); *The Lord of the Rings: A Musical Tale* (2023) and *Notes from a Small Island* (2023); *Othello* (Co-Director) and *Spike* (2022); *As You Like It* (2021); *Camelot in Concert* (2020); *Kiss Me, Kate* (2019); *Macbeth* (2019 UK Tour/2020 Wilton's Music Hall); *Sweet Charity* and *A Midsummer Night's Dream* (2018); *The Borrowers* (2017); *Twelfth Night* (2017, Wilton's Music Hall/UK Tour); *Crazy for You* (2016/2017); *Journey's End* (2014); *The Tempest* (2012); *Great Expectations* (2011) and *Heroes* (2010).

Other credits as Director include: *The Lord of the Rings: A Musical Tale* (Chicago Shakespeare Theatre, The Civic [New Zealand] and Australian Tour); *Private Peaceful* and *Pope Joan* (National Youth Theatre and West End); *Doctor Faustus* (National Theatre Studio); *Huis Clos* (Donmar Warehouse at Trafalgar Studios); *How to Find Love in Three Easy Dreams* and *Odd Jobs* (Pentabus Young Writers Festival); *The Revenger's Tragedy* (LAMDA); *Love's Labours Lost* and *The Fall of the House of Usher* (Rose Bruford College) and *Boys* (Guildford School of Speech and Drama).

As Associate Director for Propeller: *Pocket Henry V* (2014) and *Pocket Merchant* (2013); *Henry V, The Winter's Tale, Richard III, The Comedy of Errors, A Midsummer Night's Dream* and *The Merchant of Venice* (UK and International Tours).

As Resident Assistant Director at the Donmar Warehouse: *Red, Life is a Dream, A Streetcar Named Desire, A Doll's House* and *Dimetos* (2009).

Radio credits include: *Existentialism in Theatre* (BBC).

CECI CALF | Set & Costume Design

Ceci is a set and costume designer based in London. She trained at The Royal Welsh College of Music and Drama, graduating in 2018, and has since worked across the UK and Europe.

Watermill credits include: *Much Ado About Nothing* (2024) and *Othello* (2022).

Credits as Designer include: *Farm Hall* (Jermyn Street, Theatre Royal Bath, UK Tour and West End); *Comedy of Errors* (Shakespeare Theatre Company, Washington); *A Christmas Carol* (Opera Holland Park); *HIR* (Park Theatre); *The Barber of Seville* (Waterperry Festival Opera); *The Ritual Slaughter of Gorge Mastromas* and *A Skull In Connemara* (Dailes Teātris Riga, Latvia); *Breeding* (Kings Head Theatre); *Warrior Queens* (Sadler's Wells); *Waiting For Anya* and *The Mozart Question* (Barn Theatre); *Not Now, Yes So I Said Yes, How To Survive An Apocalypse, Not Quite Jerusalem* and *The Wind of Heaven* (Finborough Theatre).

Credits as Associate Designer: *Anything Is Possible If You Think About It Hard Enough* (Southwark Playhouse) and *Macbeth* (UK Tour, starring Ralph Fiennes).

CHARLY DUNFORD | Lighting Design

Charly is a graduate from Liverpool Institute for Performing Arts and was awarded the 2022 ALPD Michael Northern Award.

Watermill credits include: *Much Ado About Nothing* (2024) and *Macbeth* (2023).

Credits as Lighting Designer include: *Kinky Boots* (Chester Storyhouse); *Peak Stuff* and *Blood Harmony* (ThickSkin UK Tour); *Driftwood* (Pentabus/ThickSkin UK Tour); *this is not a crime – this is just a play* (Liverpool Everyman); *8 Hours There* and *Back* (All Things Considered UK Tour); *Danesha* (Box of Tricks UK Tour); *Sherlock Holmes: A Sign of The Four* and *Silla* (Leeds Opera Festival); *Little Red Robbin Hood* (Battersea Arts Centre); *Wild Swimming* (Theatre on the Downs); Séance (The Station); *A Very Odd Birthday Party* (UK Tour) and *Much Ado About Nothing* (Shakespeare North Playhouse).

Credits as Associate Lighting Designer include: *Fleabag* (Sherman Theatre); *Could This Place Be a Temple* (The Place); *STUFFED* (Ugly Bucket UK Tour); *Curtain Up* (Theatr Clwyd) and *The Sorcerer's Apprentice* (Northern Stage).

Credits as Assistant Lighting Designer include: *War Horse* (UK Tour); *Cabaret* (Kit Kat Club at the Playhouse) and *What's New Pussycat* (Birmingham Rep).

Credits as Relighter include: *Vortex* (Russel Maliphant Dance Company); *How Not to Drown* (ThickSkin); *Project Dictator* (Rhum and Clay); *Shades of Blue* (Matsena Productions) and *Good Grief* (Ugly Bucket).

STEVEN ATKINSON | Sound Design

Credits as Sound Designer for the RSC include: *Henry VI: Rebellion*, *Wars of the Roses*, *Maydays*, *Myth*, *The Earthworks*, *Fall of the Kingdom Rise of the Foot Soldier*, *Always Orange* and *Measure for Measure* (Stratford, UK Tour and The Barbican).

Credits as Associate Sound Designer for the RSC include: *My Neighbour Totoro* (Original Production 2022/2023) and *King Lear* (Barbican, London and BAM, New York).

Art Exhibition credits include: *Absolute Pressure* (Ribot Gallery); *A Tea Journey* (Compton Verney); *Maladapted* (Baert Gallery); *Defence Cascade* (Compton Verney); *Interview Prototype* (The Lightbox and Ingram Collection) and *Valence* (Gwangju Biennale, as Composer).

Film credits include: *Henry VI: Part One* (as Sound Supervisor).

RACHEL SAMPLEY | Projection Design

Rachel Sampley is a London-based lighting and video designer.

Watermill credits include: *The Suspicions of Mr Whicher* (2023).

Theatre credits include: *Barrier(s)* (The National Theatre); *Perfect Show for Rachel* (The Barbican); *The Great Gatsby* (Immersive – London and Seoul); *Bossy* (Zoo Co and Southbank Centre); *Cassie and the Lights* (59E59, Off Broadway, New York); *Opal Fruits* (Bristol Old Vic and Pleasance Edinburgh); *Immersive* (London, Seoul, Korea and Theatre Clwyd); *Wreckage* (Turbine Theatre) and *Breeding* (King's Head Theatre, Offie nominated for Lighting Design).

Rachel has an MA in Advanced Theatre Practice from the Royal Central School of Speech and Drama.

EMILY HOLT | Choreographer

Emily is a Choreographer and Movement Director.

Watermill credits include: *Much Ado About Nothing* (2024); *A MiniSummer Night's Dream* (2019); *Trial By Laughter* (2018); *House and Garden* (2017) and *The Wipers Times* (2016).

Theatre credits include: *A Christmas Carol (ish)* (Soho Place); *Murder for Two* (The Theatre Chipping Norton); *Killing Jack* (Queen's Theatre Hornchurch); *Shakespeare's Globe 'Celebration of The First Folio 400 Years'* (Stationer's Hall); *A Christmas Carol-ish* (Soho Theatre); *Cinderella*, *Jack & the Beanstalk* and *Dick Whittington* (Yvonne Arnaud Theatre); *The Suicide* (Storehouse); *The Entertainer* (Curve Theatre, UK Tour); *The Wipers Times* (Arts Theatre London and UK Tour); *Mr Swallow, Houdini and Mr Swallow, Dracula!* (Soho and Pleasance, Edinburgh); *The Little Beasts* (The Other Palace); *Mrs Beeton Says*, *Mother Clap's Molly House* and *Ruthless* (Mountview); *Let The Right One In*, *Bare: A Pop Opera*, *Cabaret*, *Spring Awakening* and *Fiddler On The Roof* (LAMDA).

ELSA STRACHAN | Assistant Director

Elsa trained on the MA Directing programme at Rose Bruford College, graduating with distinction in 2023.

Since then, she has worked on a variety of productions, including new writing and fresh adaptations of classic stories.

Originally from Aberdeenshire, Elsa has a passion for regional stories and is committed to making live performance accessible to audiences everywhere, believing in its power to inspire and connect communities.

Credits as Director include: *Mum* (Tramshed Theatre) and *Life on the Hyphen* (R&D, Rose Bruford College).

Credits as Assistant Director include: *Operation Epsilon* (Southwark Playhouse); *StrayDogs* (Theatre 503); *The Angry Brigade*, *Blue Stockings*, *The Welkin* and *Three Winters* (Rose Bruford College).

JACOB WU | Assistant Set & Costume Design

Jacob is a theatre designer and a scenographer from Hong Kong. He is proudly one of the Elemental Artists with the Watermill Theatre.

Jacob was trained in Scenography (MFA, Royal Central School of Speech and Drama), complementing his academic foundation in Set and Costume Design, acquired in his hometown. His work was staged at numerous venues, including the Museum of Home, Shoreditch Town Hall, and the Crypt Gallery. Jacob's performative workshop Be Right Back explores, through the lens of children, the uncertainties of a daunting world way larger than them. The piece was staged at the Stockholm Fringe Festival 2023 and won the Audience Choice Award.

Apart from his previous residency as a set designer at Chung Ying Theatre Company, Jacob has crafted site- specific installations and assisted in the design of *Giselle* for the National Ballet of Japan (2022).

Currently, Jacob serves as a Specialist Technician at Wimbledon College of Arts, UAL, where he works with students to hone their skills in model making and set design, and supervises technical workshops.

NICOLA CRAWFORD | Assistant Lighting Design

Nicola is a Lighting Designer who is excited to be working as part of the Elemental Artist programme at the Watermill Theatre.

Credits as Lighting Designer include: *The Fir Tree* (Arts Depot, London); *Flooded* (St Edmundsbury Cathedral, Bury St Edmunds); *Tiger Country* (Arts Ed, London); *The Sad Club* and *A Series of Public Apologies* (Egg Theatre, Bath); *Evermore* (The Roper Room, Bath); *Enact* (The Theatre Chipping Norton) and *Beautiful Thing* (Tobacco Factory, Bristol).

Credits as Associate Lighting Designer include: *The Artist* (Theatre Royal Plymouth); *Little Shop of Horrors* (UK Tour); *Bonnie and Clyde* (UK Tour); *A Woman Walks into a Bank* (Theatre503, London) and *The Book Thief* (Belgrade Theatre, Coventry).

Credits as Assistant Lighting Designer include: *Ain't Too Proud* (Prince Edward Theatre, London); *Bonnie and Clyde* (Garrick Theatre, London); *The Great British Bake Off Musical* (Noel Coward Theatre, London) and *Hair in Concert* (London Palladium).

Other credits include: *Pretty Woman the Musical* (UK Tour, as Deputy Head of Lighting) and *Beautiful: The Carole King Musical* (UK Tour, as Deputy Head of Lighting). NicolaCrawford.com

CHARACTERS

(if cast with 3 actors)

EDWARD FOX-INGLEBY (CAD) – 35. A charming, vain, deceitful, cynical, delusional, arrogant, callous Old Etonian politician. In other words, a Cad.

MISS CONSTANCE APPLEBY – late 20s. A prim, proper blue-stocking stenographer, who isn't afraid to challenge the Cad's most ludicrous claims. Also plays **MOTHER, WALSH-AYNSCOT, MRS BEDFORD, GERTIE, HUDSON, FORBES, GRANNY INGLEBY, FELICITY, LADY URSULA CLOPPIN, DIANA, FLORENCE** and **VIOLETTA**.

MR HENRY COLLINS – 30s. An impoverished researcher. A former Winchester pupil who is honest, bitter, frustrated and envious of the Cad, while trying to adhere to the truth. Also plays **FATHER, FREDDY DUNCATTON, CYRIL HEREWARD, BEDFORD, GERALD CHIPPENHAM, LORD OLDHAM, SIR KNIGHTON-BERRY, WINSLOW BUDDINGTON STARRET, MINISTER, OTIS WINCHESTER** and **PRIME MINISTER**.

TIME

Early twentieth century.

SETTING

The fictional county of Midhamptonshire, England.

AUTHORS' NOTES

This play is designed for a cast of three.

One actor plays the **CAD**, who is dictating his memoirs – and plays himself at various stages of his life.

One actor plays **MR COLLINS**, the researcher for the autobiography and all the other male characters from the **CAD**'s past.

One actress plays **MISS APPLEBY** the stenographer of the autobiography – and all the other female characters (and one or two male characters, as necessary) who feature in the **CAD**'s past.

However, future productions could employ a cast as large as is necessary.

HOUSE OF CADS

'I read a book...an unspeakably frivolous and cynical concoction that shows the English plutocrat without his mask. This is the face of the people whom we must overthrow.' The writer is Josef Goebbels, Hitler's Minister for Propaganda, in his diary entry for 8 December 1940. He was referring to the memoirs of Edward Fox-Ingleby, a Tory politician who, after Eton and Oxford (naturally), rose through the ranks of the party by lying, cheating and sleeping his way to the top. Unbeknown to Goebbels, Fox-Ingleby was a fiction – the antihero of a satirical novel by Scottish writer A.G. Macdonell – *The Autobiography of a Cad*.

Published in 1938, the book was not a commercial success. As war broke out the public had no appetite for reading about their degenerate leaders – however darkly comical. The Cad sank without trace – until now. Ian Hislop and I have brought the rotter back to life, in all his absurd, delusional and mendacious glory.

Fox-Ingleby's is an archetypal political memoir – score-settling, pompous and a celebration of self: self-regarding, self-serving and self-pitying. The only self it doesn't feature is awareness. He deplores the vanity of autobiographers, but luckily vanity 'is not, and never has been, one of my weaknesses.'

For a book written over 80 years ago it is remarkably topical. There are similarities to a number of subsequent memoirs and diaries – notably those of Alan Clark, a minister under Margaret Thatcher. Fox-Ingleby has contempt for the working classes, despising the 'stupidity and cunning' of 'peasants' – while Clark wondered whether he'd get sacked for urinating out of the window of his minister's office and 'spattering the ant-like minions below.'

Fox-Ingleby's lechery is unconfined, pursuing shopgirls, actresses and the wives of friends and superiors. Clark, meanwhile, lusted after his boss. 'By God, she is so beautiful,' he wrote of Prime Minister Margaret Thatcher. '...still bewitching as Eva Peron must have been... I radiated protective feelings – and indeed feelings of another kind.'

The Cad is also reminiscent of the diaries of Tory MP Henry 'Chips' Channon, with his malicious snobbery and louche disregard for social mores. Channon detailed his affairs with everyone – including playwright Terence Rattigan – as well as spankings and his fondness for Nazis.

Channon's words are unminced. He describes the new king Edward VIII leaping to his feet during dinner, announcing: 'I want to pump shit.' Fox-Ingleby is more polite about Royalty – but only because he has hopes for the gong he feels he undoubtedly deserves.

Written with an eye on posterity, political memoirs are more economical with the truth than diaries. Liz Truss's *Ten Years To Save the West* blames everyone except herself, who, far from crashing the economy, 'was seeking to conduct a handbrake turn to avoid driving off the edge.' Critics are 'untruthers', her ousting is by a mysterious elite – a.k.a. 'The Blob'.

Meanwhile the memoir of Truss's predecessor – *Boris Johnson Unleashed* – unleashes his achievements, but not his numerous affairs. The Cad, however, combines the diarist's candour with the memoirist's self-certainty. He is revealing about his sexual escapades (but never in the wrong) and bullish about his place in history (and always in the right).

In his conclusion, following a spate of career-threatening scandals, Fox-Ingleby presages Johnson's boosterish valedictory speech outside Number Ten. See if you can tell them apart. 'I am proud to have discharged the promises I made my party...' said one. 'Together we have laid foundations that will stand the test of time.' And the other: 'Do not forget...that I helped to make Britain a better place to live in... And above all...a better place for women to live in.' The first is Johnson, the second the Cad. And both reference the classics to reinforce their gravitas. While Johnson compares himself to Cincinnatus, returning to his plough, Fox-Ingleby as Minister of Fine Arts likens himself to Pericles, laying down a 'broad basis for a new national culture' (by censoring anything liberal and axing the arts).

The late journalist and broadcaster Simon Hoggart wrote an introduction to this 'magnificently abusive satire', in which he declared it 'as fresh as tomorrow's front page' and funnier than Macdonell's most famous comic creation, *England their England*, with its famed cricket match. 'Obviously the character is a monstrous grotesque. But we can still meet his descendants today.' Hoggart likens him to Jonathan Aitken MP (jailed for perjury) and Neil Hamilton MP (disgraced in the Cash for Questions scandal). The Cad shows that standards were declining long before the arrival of the Thatcherite chancers.

Like his satirical masterpiece, Archibald Gordon Macdonell has largely been forgotten. He is buried in Wolvercote Cemetery along with J.R.R. Tolkien – but unlike the well-maintained shrine to the *Lord of the Rings* author, Macdonell's grave is sadly neglected.

Born in Poona (now Pune) in 1895, he died in 1941. In his 45 years he produced 19 books, short stories, Cowardesque West End comedies – while working as a drama critic and parliamentary sketch writer. Macdonell also stood twice as a Liberal candidate in Lincoln (defeated both times) – so was well-placed to observe politicians at close quarters.

Fox-Ingleby is the antithesis of Macdonell. A Great War shirker (Macdonell served on the front line and was invalided out) a despiser of the League of Nations (Macdonell spent 5 years working there) and an old Etonian who is withering about Winchester College (of which Macdonell was a pupil). A Winchester alumnus once said, 'Wykehamists write the speeches, Etonians make them' – which may be the source of Macdonell's antipathy.

The inspiration for the novel may have been Mary Dunn's *Lady Addle Remembers* (1936), which Macdonell reviewed with great enthusiasm – 'a treasure – a neat, ironic, swift, bantering wit.' Lady Addle was a caricature of an aristocratic Victorian lady, whose family was full of eccentrics like Sir Ludovic FitzTartan. His hobbies included cockroach racing and shooting bees. Like the Cad, Lady Addle is a convincing, if more whimsical creation. Fox-Ingleby is altogether darker and bleaker.

There are challenges to staging the Cad. Actual arts funding cuts necessitated a cast of just three. Macdonell's 'picaresque' approach to storytelling meant creating a dramatic plot. Above all, this awful character had to be someone you would want to spend two hours with in a theatre. Hopefully, the audience will succumb to the outrageous charm of this precursor to Flashman, and become complicit in the misdemeanours of the prototype Alan B'Stard. The Cad is appalling, but like Patricia Highsmith's *Talented Mr Ripley* – appealing. You end up willing him to succeed. Whether he does or not, you will have to see the play to find out.

Nick Newman

(A version of this article first appeared in *The Sunday Times*)

ACT ONE

Scene One

(Onstage in the spotlight is a lectern. Back projected we see a newspaper headline from the 1920s: 'BELEAGUERED FOX-INGLEBY MP TO MAKE STATEMENT'. The **CAD** *appears. He is a typical politician – sombre, earnest, shifty and yet charming. We hear the sound of flashbulbs and cameras clicking.)*

CAD. Ladies and Gentlemen it is with a heavy heart that I address you this afternoon. In recent weeks I have been the victim of rumours and gossip bordering on character assassination. These smears are as false as they are egregious. I have even been called the 'C' word. Not a 'Conservative'. No. A 'Cad'. I acknowledge that I may have become a distraction from the very important business of government. So I have reflected on my record and examined my own conscience – and after much careful consideration I have decided to...

(The **CAD** *then steps away from the lectern and addresses the audience directly. We are now in the present.)*

(To audience.) ...but I'm getting ahead of myself. It is important to tell the story from the beginning. For the benefit of posterity I always knew that I owed it to you, the people, to produce my memoirs in full. So I had embarked on the telling of my remarkable life, provisionally to be titled The Autobiography of a...

(Pause.)

CAD. Political Titan.

Scene Two

*(The female stenographer, **MISS APPLEBY**, is sitting at a desk to the side of the stage taking notes.)*

(We are observing the writing process of the Cad's autobiography, taking place in the Cad's study.)

*(There is also a wardrobe, from which the **CAD** will take various garments for costume changes when we go into flashbacks from **CAD**'s past. A chaise longue and screen complete the furniture. Throughout, back-projected Newspaper Headlines set the historical scene.)*

MISS APPLEBY. 'The Autobiography of a Political Titan.' Is that still the working title?

CAD. Unless you think it's too self-deprecating?

MISS APPLEBY. *(Laughs.)* No. I don't think it is.

CAD. Good. So let's stick with that Miss Appleby. I had another idea for the opening paragraph…

*(**MISS APPLEBY** sighs. She puts more paper in the machine.)*

MISS APPLEBY. Page one, draft seventeen

CAD. *(Dictating.)* 'All great men in the rich pageant of Britain's island history find that there are those lesser mortals who relish the opportunity to diminish their achievements and legacy. But this is not their story. It is *mine*. Have you got all that?

MISS APPLEBY. Your story. No-one else's.

CAD. And underline 'mine'.

MISS APPLEBY. Obviously.

CAD. *(Continuing to dictate.)* It is the inspiring tale of one Edward Percival Fox-Ingleby of the Midhamptonshire Fox-Inglebys...

> *(Enter* **MR COLLINS**. **MR COLLINS**, *about thirty-five, with a dusty old book. He is a hired researcher for the autobiography.)*

MR COLLINS. Yes, I've been checking on the origins of the Fox-Ingleby lineage and the name doesn't seem to go back beyond the mid-Nineteenth Century.

CAD. Nonsense, Mr Collins. I don't pay you as a researcher to undermine my genealogy...

MR COLLINS. You haven't paid me at all sir.

CAD. Is it not reward enough that you are privy to the insight and wisdom of one of your country's leading political figures. Surely it is you who should be paying *me* for the extraordinary opportunity I have given you.

MR COLLINS. I have to say that I am lost for words.

CAD. Which is why I am a successful man of letters and you are a somewhat desperate scribbler who will always struggle to make a living out of your impenetrable poetry and overwrought prose.

MR COLLINS. That's unfair.

CAD. Like the omission of the Fox-Inglebys from the Domesday Book. It's an outrage! We *definitely* came over with William the Conqueror.

MR COLLINS. Though there is no mention of your family in the roll of honour at Battle Abbey.

CAD. Details, details, Mr Collins! My family tree is strong and sturdy.

> *(He whacks a riding crop down on the desk to terminate the discussion.)*

MR COLLINS. *(Consulting tome.)* Though some branches appear to have fallen off. And I'm afraid I've discovered some gaps in the foliage.

CAD. Minor gaps. Trivial gaps. The tree is sound! Fine old English oak!

MR COLLINS. I can't find any mention of the Inglebys until the Battle of Agincourt in 1415 when there IS an English soldier recorded called Inglebourne.

CAD. That's the fellow! Flower of chivalry. Leading the charge.

> *(He hold the riding crop like a sabre leading the charge and performs some imaginary swordplay.)*
>
> *(**MR COLLINS** shows him book.)*

MR COLLINS. He was hanged for pilfering from the dead.

CAD. That's what his enemies would *want* you to believe. An heroic figure, undoubtedly. I'm afraid Mr Collins you need to work harder, and find some better sources.

MR COLLINS. From my research your family story really begins with your Grandfather who, despite his later fortune, came from a very humble background.

CAD. That is where you're wrong. The fact that my grandfather Jedediah had no inheritance leads me to suspect that *his* father – my Great Grandfather – must have gambled away the Ingleby millions in the Hell-Fire Club, in the company of Fox, Pitt, Sheridan and The Prince Regent.

MR COLLINS. Do you have any evidence for that?

CAD. None. But it is the only possible explanation for Grandpapa Jedediah's impecunious beginnings. So get out and prove it!

> *(**CAD** sends **MR COLLINS** packing, throwing the book after him.)*

CAD. *(To* **MISS APPLEBY.***)* Now, we must address another relative who is sadly a lot less eminent. My Father. However deep my grievances against Papa, and no matter how unfairly he treated me, I will not hear a word against him.

> *(Spotlight on* **CAD** *addressing audience allows actors playing* **MR COLLINS** *and* **MISS APPLEBY** *to exit and change.)*

(To audience.) The trouble with Father was that he was a saint. Of the worst kind. He was an *amateur* saint. God knows, professional saints are pretty awful, but amateurs – whether in sanctification or theatricals – are unbearably worse. And my mother was even worse than my father.

Scene Three

(Enter **FATHER** *sporting moustache.* **MOTHER** *with basket of provisions for the poor. We are now in flashback.)*

FATHER. Good day to you, good day to you all. Yes, I'll be reroofing those leaky cottages – and yes, I'll be rebuilding those old barns for the tenant farmers.

MOTHER. And we will be laying on water and gas for the estate, maintaining fences and gates and paying for hedging and ditching.

CAD. *(To audience.)* Aren't they ghastly?

FATHER. I will forego payment of your annual rent this year on the grounds that the harvest has been ruined by the weather...

CAD. *(To audience.)* Have you heard of anything like it?

MOTHER. I have clothes, boots and sacks of coal for everyone.

CAD. *(To audience.)* No wonder they were the laughing-stock of the county. I loved my mother dearly, and in her own fussy way she was wonderful and well-meaning but she was so generous to the tenants that it was hardly necessary for them to do any work at all!

MOTHER. Congratulations, Mrs Cooper, another baby... I'll bring some blankets and send the doctor round immediately.

CAD. *(To audience.)* She was a positive encouragement to idleness and plebeian incontinence! But it is not for me to criticise.

She was, however, a Fox – and descended, I believe, from Gaston de Foix, who features, you will remember in the fourteenth century Froissart Chronicles.

Scene Four

*(Enter **MR COLLINS**, with copy of the Froissart Chronicles. We are back in the present.)*

MR COLLINS. Yes, I'm having difficulty finding a direct link with Froissart...

CAD. I sometimes wonder if you're up to this job. There are a lot of unemployed men out there – not the fault of this government – who would relish the opportunity that you have been given. Instead you repeatedly attempt to plant seeds of doubt about every simple biographical detail.

MR COLLINS. *(Wearily.)* I'll look through the Chronicles again. I'm sure it's in there somewhere.

CAD. *I'm* sure it is too. And that's what counts. And now we must turn to my time at Eton.

MR COLLINS. Must we?

CAD. We must.

MR COLLINS. I am surprised it has taken so long.

*(Raises his eyebrows at **MISS APPLEBY**, who ignores him.)*

MISS APPLEBY. Was it all terribly beastly?

CAD. *(To **MISS APPLEBY**.)* It is customary in major autobiographies of this nature for the subject to give an account of their formative years. It is now fashionable to recount the sufferings and miseries of one's schooldays. So for the record... I LOVED every minute!

(Back projection depicts Eton College.)

(To audience.) I was young, I was rich, I was clever, I was good looking and I acquired a circle of friends that was to last me the rest of my life.

(Sound of boys singing the "Eton Boating Song" in background.)

BOYS.
> JOLLY BOATING WEATHER,
> AND A HAY HARVEST BREEZE,
> BLADE ON THE FEATHER,
> SHADE OFF THE TREES,
> SWING SWING TOGETHER,
> WITH YOUR BODIES BETWEEN YOUR KNEES,
> SWING SWING TOGETHER,
> WITH YOUR BODIES BETWEEN YOUR KNEES.

CAD. *(Over song.)* Lord Plaistow, Le Comte de St Etienne de La Fosse, Lord Bletchley, good old Freddy Duncatton, Charlie Hudson whose father was Chairman of the Pacific Insurance Company and Harry Walsh-Aynscot who was heir to a Zinc fortune...

MR COLLINS. And what drew you to this disparate group of random young men?

CAD. We shared a taste for the elegancies of life and a distaste for cricket, schoolmasters and the lower classes.

MISS APPLEBY. Are you sure you want to include that last observation?

CAD. Perhaps you're right. We don't want to alienate the cricket-loving reader.

MR COLLINS. Did you not enjoy playing games?

CAD. Heavens no. I was a wet bob!

MISS APPLEBY. What is a wet bob?

CAD. Really, young people today don't know anything. A wet bob is someone who rows – as opposed to a dry bob, who is a muddied oaf who runs about chasing balls.

MR COLLINS. So did you row for the school?

CAD. No. I rowed in a small boat for pleasure! With one other person and a bottle or two of something for refreshment. Ah, happy days...

MR COLLINS. Your time at Eton sounds all-too idyllic.

CAD. That's because you had the misfortune of going to Winchester, Mr Collins.

> (**MR COLLINS** *exits [to allow actor to change].*)

MISS APPLEBY. But what about the discipline, and corporal punishment? I've heard stories of severe beatings.

CAD. Yes, there were beatings.

> (*Pause.*)

I beat *everyone* I could!

The sons of the nouveau riche, the sons of jumped-up nabobs, the sons of dreary country parsons... one almost got tired of beating bourgeois posteriors!

> (**MISS APPLEBY** *looks shocked.*)

I *joke* of course!

> (**MISS APPLEBY** *looks relieved.*)

I *NEVER* got tired of it!

> (*He whacks at imaginary posteriors all around him with riding crop.*)

Take that, Fenton Minor, you ghastly oik! Six of the best for having a father in trade!

MISS APPLEBY. How does your illustrious Eton chapter end?

CAD. At Oxford of course!

> (**MISS APPLEBY** *also exits to change.*)

(To audience.) Ah, the dreaming spires. The ancient seat of learning where a whole new world opened up, which I was privileged to share with new Oxford pals, Lord Plaistow, Le Comte de St Etienne de La Fosse, Lord Bletchley, Charlie Hudson whose father was Chairman of the Pacific Insurance Company and Harry Walsh-Aynscot who was heir to a Zinc fortune...and of course, good old Freddy Duncatton...

Scene Five

(We hear sound of bells, choirs and see back projection of dreaming spires as **CAD** *dons mortarboard and gown. He proceeds to open a bottle of champagne. We are in flashback.)*

(Another student wearing mortarboard and gown enters. The actor playing **MR COLLINS** *is now Cad's oldest friend,* **FREDDY DUNCATTON**.*)*

DUNCATTON. Congratulations Fox-Ingleby! You're officially in!

CAD. Freddy, this is unquestionably the most wonderful day of my life! To receive the approbation of one's peers is the summit of human achievement.

*(***DUNCATTON*** hands him a fancy waistcoat, which he puts on.)*

DUNCATTON. Welcome to the Bullingdon Club!

(He hands him his fancy Bullingdon Club coat.)

CAD & DUNCATTON. Buller Buller Buller!

(They engage in the Bullingdon Club stomp.)

(Enter **WALSH-AYNSCOT** *also wearing Bullingdon attire. Actress playing* **MISS APPLEBY** *is now* **WALSH-AYNSCOT**.*)*

CAD. What ho, Walsh-Aynscot!

WALSH-AYNSCOT. I'm sorry old man, I've just heard the news.

DUNCATTON. Isn't it splendid? Edward's been admitted! Buller Buller Buller! Fizzington all round!

WALSH-AYNSCOT. *(Sombre.)* No – about your parents, Edward. The porter just told me.

DUNCATTON. What?

CAD. Oh yes. I received some very bad news.

There was a terrible train crash on the Midland Railway Line. Mother and Father were on board.

DUNCATTON. Dear God.

CAD. And I'm afraid they lost their lives.

DUNCATTON. When did this happen?

CAD. This morning.

(A moment of sombre reflection. **DUNCATTON** *pats* **CAD***'s shoulder.)*

DUNCATTON. Condolences, old pal.

WALSH-AYNSCOT. Grim show.

CAD. Condolences accepted.

But passionate weeping will not turn back the hands of time. My loss is irreparable, but my duty is to the future, not the past!

ALL. Quite so. Bravely said.

CAD. As Diomedes put it 'Like the leaves of the forest, so are the generations of men.'

ALL. Noble sentiments.

(The action freezes onstage, as **CAD** *comes out of the scene to address the audience.)*

CAD. *(To audience.)* I fear that the reader at this juncture might start getting judgemental and question the extent of my profound grief at the expiry of my dear and...quite annoying parents on their way to open a Liberal Party Bazaar and Jumble Sale.

(Pause.)

CAD. In Wolverhampton! Of all places?! But believe me, there was nothing to be gained by pretending that Mother and Father had not outstayed their utility.

(Action resumes.)

(To **STUDENTS.***)* Life must go on! And I intend to live it!

(Pours more champagne for all.)

DUNCATTON. Quite right!

WALSH-AYNSCOT. Here's to you Edward!

(They toast him.)

CAD. And to my mind in such circumstances there is only one appropriate response.

(Beat.)

We must trash the Senior Tutor's rooms!

(Big cheer from all.)

ALL. Buller Buller Buller!

(The **THREE** *of them dance round singing while placing items from the Senior Tutor's study in a pile in the centre.)*

(They sing the "Buller Song." **CAD** *conducts the singing with a riding crop.)*

BULLER BULLER BULLER,
LET THE OIKIES SCOFF,
BULLER BULLER BULLER,
WE'LL PULL THEIR TROUSERS OFF!
BULLER BULLER BULLER
LET THE TOWNIES QUIVER
BULLER BULLER BULLER

THROW THEM IN THE RIVER!
BULLER BULLER BULLER
PLEBS GET OUT THE WAY,
BULLER BULLER BULLER
WE'LL RULE THE WORLD ONE DAY

> *(They throw on the fire many books and papers, they smash pots, and put their heads through paintings covering everything in paint before setting fire to it.* **DUNCATTON** *and* **WALSH-AYNSCOT** *dance off.)*

CAD. *(To audience.)* This was the moment when I encountered what can only be described as my nemesis – or Cyril Hereward as he preferred to be called. A fellow student who will feature prominently in the rest of this narrative.

> *(Enter* **HEREWARD/MR COLLINS**, *wearing spectacles and a dressing gown.)*

HEREWARD. What on earth are you doing?

CAD. We're setting fire to the Prof's verse translation of Lucretius, of course!

HEREWARD. He's been working on it for seventeen years!

CAD. In that case it should be a lot better. Frightful bilge!

HEREWARD. No it's not. And you should stop at once before I call the authorities.

CAD. I don't care for your tone. Or indeed your face.

> *(***CAD*** whacks him across the face with a riding crop, knocking off his spectacles.)*

(To audience.) For some inexplicable reason he held this trivial incident against me for the rest of his life. Surely he must have understood that his face was simply too inviting a temptation to anyone who happened to have a riding crop in his hand.

HEREWARD. You unspeakable swine, Fox-Ingleby!

CAD. *(To audience.)* The only blame that could possibly attach to me is that I acted impulsively. He was taller than me – six foot four as I recall – and you could argue that I was being foolhardy in defending myself against such an opponent.

> (**HEREWARD** *is clearly not six foot four, but is reeling from shock, trying to find his spectacles on the floor.* **HEREWARD** *exits.*)

(To audience.) I decided at this point that a tactical retreat was in order.

> (**CAD** *runs for it, ducking round the stage.*)

> (*While running on the spot.*)

I therefore managed to evade capture by the Dean and the Proctors when the cowardly Hereward called them in. My Buller colleagues were not so fortunate.

Scene Six

(Enter **WALSH-AYNSCOT/MISS APPLEBY** *and* **DUNCATTON/MR COLLINS** *who start clearing up the stage.)*

WALSH-AYNSCOT. Expelled! We've been sent down!

DUNCATTON. And fined fifty guineas!

CAD. That is bad luck

WALSH-AYNSCOT. What did you get?

CAD. Er… I got…away with it. I managed to avoid all penalties on the grounds of not being there when you were unfortunately caught. Sorry!

DUNCATTON. You utter bounder!

CAD. I thought you would be happy for me. I thought you were better friends than this but obviously I was mistaken.

WALSH-AYNSCOT. You got us into it. It was your idea. And now *we've* got the boot.

CAD. I thought you'd accept your fate, say 'Justice is justice' and 'dear old Edward has escaped and good luck to him!' But no.

WALSH-AYNSCOT. You really are beyond the pale, Fox-Ingleby.

CAD. I had you two down as good chaps but it turns out you're not as good as I'd thought. Clearly the bonds of fellowship are not as sacrosanct as a gentleman might hope to expect. Alas for human nature.

DUNCATTON. Bit harsh Fox-Ingleby!

CAD. No, no, if that's what you want I shall go and tell the Dean that it was all my fault, I was entirely to blame and I will accept all the punishment myself. And then I shall tell my parents… oh no, I shan't on account of the fact that they are dead, and I am an orphan.

DUNCATTON. Sorry old man, I forgot.

WALSH-AYNSCOT. No need to do anything rash. We're in the soup – no need to all drown in it.

CAD. *(To audience.)* Jolly decent of Walsh-Aynscot. But that was Walsh-Aynscot all over – always trying to do the decent thing. Like when he took full responsibility for that giggly Oxford shopgirl's baby and paid off her grasping parents. Naturally he got a bit of a shock when the infant popped out looking suspiciously like yours truly. How I laughed!

> *(***CAD*** turns to audience and gives a big thumbs up. Flashback ends.)*

Scene Seven

(Back in the present, with **CAD, MISS APPLEBY** *and* **MR COLLINS**.*)*

MISS APPLEBY. So for the record, your time at Oxford was a riot of youthful high jinks.

CAD. ...and the odd flirtation with game young fillies from the town. Wild oats may have been sown. Ha ha ha!

MISS APPLEBY. I'm not entirely sure the reader will share your amusement. Times have changed and your attitudes to women are no longer acceptable.

CAD. I'm sorry.

MISS APPLEBY. Thank you.

CAD. I'm sorry if that's what you think, but you are quite wrong. I of course acted honourably at all times – unlike some of my contemporaries. If I have a fault, it is that I am *too* honourable.

(To audience.) Walsh-Aynscot, was, as the heir to a Zinc fortune, a much better prospective father to the unfortunate mite than yours truly. I was doing everybody a favour. Sadly Walsh-Aynscot didn't see it that way and had the temerity to ask ME for money! I said 'over my dead body'. Which was ironic as it was HE who was killed on the first day of the Somme! They say that war is hell – but for me it was something of a blessing!

(Back in the present.)

MISS APPLEBY. So to be absolutely clear, are we saying that you don't have a problem with women?

CAD. I have never had a problem with women. The fairer sex found me irresistible. Still do. Can't help it.

MISS APPLEBY. Oh really! Please take it from me that you are not irresistible.

CAD. Methinks the lady doth protest too much!

(**MISS APPLEBY** *is embarrassed.*)

Macbeth

MR COLLINS. I think you'll find it's Hamlet

CAD. And I think *you'll* find you spent too much time in the college library cramming for a miserable first when you should have been out savouring the sap-rising joys of the lusty season of youth.

(**MISS APPLEBY** *rolls eyes in disapproval.*)

In an honourable way.

No, let's settle this now – where's my Shakespeare?

(*He leaves, leaving* **MR COLLINS** *and* **MISS APPLEBY** *alone. Awkward silence. Whispered conversation.*)

MISS APPLEBY. Good for you for standing up to him

MR COLLINS. Someone has to. It's all bit pathetic, isn't it? A bit desperate?

MISS APPLEBY. I suppose he is fighting for his political life.

MR COLLINS. So we had better get on with this book before it's too late...

(**CAD** *returns with copy of Shakespeare.*)

CAD. Yes thought so, it WAS Hamlet as I said. Told you so.

MR COLLINS. But...

CAD. I'm sorry, I'm a stickler for the truth...

(*He tosses the tome to* **MR COLLINS** *who is open-mouthed.*)

...and the truth is, Mr Collins, I had more fun at Oxford than you did. And remembered more Shakespeare, apparently!

MISS APPLEBY. Shall we press on?

MR COLLINS. You say you weren't *expelled* from Oxford but according to the University Gazette you DID leave Oriel College without a degree.

CAD. Yes, some people need a first class degree to prove their intellectual capabilities, but I always knew that academic honours mean little when judging the fineness of the brain of those born naturally clever.

MR COLLINS. You failed your exams, didn't you?

*(Action freezes, as **CAD** addresses audience.)*

CAD. *(To audience.)* No, Swotty Wilkinson failed my exams, despite being paid handsomely to take them in my place. All he succeeded in doing was getting caught. Damn fool! And people said he was clever. I had to tell the Dons it was all a terrible misunderstanding and buy the college a new library – with a wine cellar underneath, for the senior common room. Allowed me to leave with honour and a bronze plaque on the wall.

(Action unfreezes.)

(To **MR COLLINS.***)* I had to leave Oxford as I found the duties of my recently inherited estate too onerous. And so, sadly, I put the needs of my tenants and workers above my own scholarly ambitions. And to be honest, there was much work to be done on the Grantly Estate...

*(***MR COLLINS** *exits.* **CAD** *begins to change into hunting pink and a riding hat.)*

Scene Eight

(Flashback. We are in the past when the **CAD** *returned to take over Grantly Manor.)*

CAD. *(Blows horn.)* Tally ho!

(To audience.) My dear departed parents had left Grantly Manor in a parlous state having banned hunting through some squeamish concern for the fox. The only fox I was concerned about was the Fox-Ingleby who was now in charge.

(Enter **BEDFORD/MR COLLINS**, *the Estate Manager. He is an elderly, kindly figure.)*

BEDFORD. Welcome back, young Sir.

CAD. Ah Bedford! How goes the estate managing mallarkey?

BEDFORD. You'll find everything in good order Sir.

CAD. Nonsense! My parents overpaid the workers and squandered hundreds of pounds on their accommodation. As a result they are all lazy and feckless.

BEDFORD. They are here now Sir.

(He indicates off.)

*(***CAD*** turns to address his tenants offstage.)*

CAD. What a pleasure to see you all again. You will no doubt agree that my Father's management style was somewhat wanting, not to say Socialist and borderline Bolshevik.

BEDFORD. We will not see his like again.

CAD. No you certainly won't! Now Mr Bedford – the wages on this estate are a disgrace.

BEDFORD. You think so Sir?

CAD. Yes – they are far too high. From now on we will pay a maximum wage...

> *(Murmurs of delight.)*

...of the minimum wage that everyone else is paying. What could be fairer than that?

> *(Murmurs of dissent.)*

Anything else? That fox isn't going to hunt itself!

> *(He blows horn again.)*

BEDFORD. About the cottages, Sir. The roofs need to be repaired.

CAD. And they will be...

> *(Murmurs of delight.)*

By the tenants themselves!

> *(Murmurs of dissent.)*

I'm glad you agree! There's nothing like a drip, drip drip of rainwater on the head to motivate your average labourer Johnny to pull his finger out and get on with some home improvements.

> *(Murmurs of dissent.)*

> *(Another blow on the horn.)*

View hallooo!

(To audience.) Yes, I've always had a gift for motivating the yokels of the rural proletariat.

> *(Enter **MRS BEDFORD/MISS APPLEBY**, breathless.)*

Who are you?

MRS BEDFORD. Mrs Bedford, Sir.

CAD. And what do you want?

MRS BEDFORD. The common land beyond the wall's caught fire!

CAD. I fail to see why that should be of any concern to myself, Mrs Bedford. I entirely respect the ancient rights of the commoners to look after their own land.

(The fire offstage is growing in intensity.)

MRS BEDFORD. The wind is from the north east, sir. And the fire is sweeping towards *your* beech wood.

*(**CAD** suddenly leaps into panic mode.)*

CAD. Why didn't you tell me sooner? Bedford – what are you going to do?

BEDFORD. I haven't got enough hands. I'll have to go the village to find some more men to help put out the fire.

CAD. Then be quick about it! Offer them half a crown – that should encourage their sense of public duty!

*(**BEDFORD** leaves, as the sound of fire increases. **CAD** and **MRS BEDFORD** watch from afar.)*

MRS BEDFORD. It's almost at the trees...but there's William with the Venables boys...and the Harris family...and old man Cooper with a bucket...

CAD. *(Shouting off.)* Put your backs into it lads! Think of my beautiful beech woods! I know you're familiar with them – half of you have been poaching there!

MRS BEDFORD. Thank the Lord – the wind's changed! It's blowing the fire back onto the common.

CAD. That's a relief!

MRS BEDFORD. Your wood's safe Mister Fox-Ingleby!

CAD. Unlike the common land which seems to be scorched. Oh well. There we go. All's well that ends well!

> (**BEDFORD** *enters, sweaty and covered in soot.*)

BEDFORD. The fire is dying away of its own accord Sir.

CAD. Excellent! Give the men a shilling apiece and my warmest thanks.

BEDFORD. You promised half a crown Sir.

CAD. Yes, but in the circumstances it would have been absurd to have paid out half a crown for half an hour's work.

MRS BEDFORD. That's not right Sir. A promise is a promise.

CAD. Not if the circumstances alter.

BEDFORD. The villagers are a good lot. They loved your father, and I don't want to see you get wrong with them for the matter of a few shillings. Please Sir!

> (**BEDFORD** *grabs his arm pleadingly.*)

CAD. Careful with my hunting jacket – it's Savile Row – and your hands are covered in bucolic detritus!

MRS BEDFORD. It's not fair Sir!

BEDFORD. And I've already paid the men out of my own pocket.

> (**CAD** *laughs.*)

CAD. Ha! You cunning old rascal! All this concern for my good name and honour was simply to get your own money back! Be off with you!

> (**CAD** *chases* **BEDFORD** *off with his riding crop.*)

MRS BEDFORD. No, Sir, William was just…

CAD. I know perfectly well what the old rogue was trying to do! Make the men think what a terrific chap he is and what a bounder I am!

MRS BEDFORD. But what about William's money?

CAD. We shall say no more about it. I forgive him.

(Flashback ends. Back in the present.)

Scene Nine

CAD. *(To* **MR COLLINS.***)* ...and that was how I quelled the Great Grantly Manor Peasants' Revolt! But I don't want you to think too harshly of old Bedford. He was a decent old cock – but like peasants the world over he combined the qualities of cunning, strength and stupidity. Hence their inevitable defeat when confronted by a noble descendant of the conquering Norman Fox-Inglebys!

MR COLLINS. I still haven't managed to establish that direct lineage yet.

CAD. I'm sure you will!

MR COLLINS. As well as attempting to identify the exact roots of your family tree, I have been examining the estate accounts on the land registry.

CAD. Was that in your remit?

MR COLLINS. I thought it might be of historical interest.

CAD. As indeed might be the contents of my dustbins. But I think we can spare the reader the details of what I drank for dinner last night.

MR COLLINS. Nonetheless, given that the rents from your estate were quite significant at this period, why were you so...'economically stringent' with your workers?

CAD. The problem was, I was too generous elsewhere. Which was why I often found myself a little short of funds through no fault of my own.

MR COLLINS. So whose fault was it?

CAD. It seems ungentlemanly to say it but the fault lay entirely with the ladies.

MISS APPLEBY. Really?

CAD. I'm afraid so. From the moment I left Bedford in charge of Grantly Manor and took up residence in my chambers in Albany, I became the victim of a succession of women who exploited my weakness for the fairer sex.

MISS APPLEBY. Poor you!

CAD. I know. But it is a cross I have to bear. Have you any idea how much orchids cost before the war? Or an account at a decent Bond Street jeweller? Or how much it cost to keep the Stage Doorkeeper of a West End Theatre sweet?

MISS APPLEBY. My heart bleeds for you. Can one assume that all these ladies were Chorus Girls?

CAD. You assume wrong, Miss Appleby! Some of them had small speaking parts!

Though obviously the more famous actresses were reserved for his Majesty the King. Noblesse oblige!

(**MR COLLINS** *drops his papers in shock.*)

(*To* **MISS APPLEBY**.) Perhaps we shall strike that from the record – a gentleman always keeps confidences, and out of loyalty to the Crown I don't want to ruin my chances of any honour that the new King might wish to bestow on me. The Order of the Garter would be most acceptable – and arguably no less than I deserve. But that is not for me to judge.

(*To audience.*) The thing was, the second and third rows of the chorus were easy game for a rich young bachelor. We all had discreet establishments in unfashionable Maida Vale where we installed what we called these 'mistresses of the moment'. But they were damned pricey – which meant I had to keep yokel expenses to a minimum.

Scene Ten

(Flashback. Champagne cork pops. We hear wind up gramophone playing "La Vie Parisienne.")

*(**CAD** starts unbuttoning his shirt, removing his braces, taking off his shoes.)*

CAD. I'm afraid I can't be long as I have to be at the Beefsteak Club for dinner.

*(Enter **GERTIE** in state of undress.)*

GERTIE. You promised to take me out for dinner.

CAD. Sorry, the Beefsteak Club's chaps only. And anyway, I thought you were onstage at the Gaiety this evening?

GERTIE. I think you're confusing me with someone else.

CAD. Of course I'm not, Irene.

GERTIE. I'm not Irene.

CAD. I know that! I'm teasing you, Beryl.

GERTIE. I'm not Beryl.

CAD. Lottie? Kitty? Olive?

GERTIE. I'm Gertie.

CAD. Of course you are. Gertie. Dear sweet Gertie with the smiling eyes.

GERTIE. You do love me don't you Edward?

CAD. Of course I love you. From the moment I saw you in 'The Runaway Girl'.

GERTIE. I wasn't in that. I was in 'Our Miss Gibbs'.

CAD. And very good you were too.

GERTIE. Was I really?

CAD. You lit up the stage.

> *(To audience.)* There always comes a difficult moment in these relationships when you both know it's all over – except one of you doesn't.

> *(To* **GERTIE.***)* Dear darling Gertie, all good things must come to an end...

GERTIE. Must they?

CAD. Yes they must. And when they do, it's best to admit that it's sad but inevitable, and as adults, part on the best of terms.

GERTIE. *(In tears.)* Are you saying...it's over?

CAD. Not immediately. I still have time before dinner to say goodbye properly.

> *(He starts undoing his trousers.)*

GERTIE. But you said you loved me...you wrote me those wonderful intimate letters.

CAD. Ah yes, the letters. I think it would be better all round if you gave them back to me.

GERTIE. I want to keep them forever as a memory of our time together.

CAD. That's sweet, Gertie old thing – but I think you'll find that legally they are MY copyright.

GERTIE. Dear Edward, I think *you'll* find that legally they are MY property as the recipient and I am at liberty to share them with anyone.

CAD. Ha! You sound like a lawyer, dearest, rather than the divine bubbly chanteuse who captured my heart.

> *(Beat.)*

How much do you want? £100? £200?

GERTIE. Money cannot buy such precious memories.

CAD. All right – £300 and that's it.

GERTIE. They were so personal. Such detail.

CAD. £500 and that's the end of the matter.

GERTIE. Done.

> *(They shake hands. He gives her the money.)*

I just have one further request. I can keep the diamonds, can't I darling?

CAD. Of course you must keep the diamonds. That's completely different from the letters. You must look at them and think of your darling Mister Foxy.

> *(They embrace. She slips off.)*

(To audience.) There was no way I was going to let the scheming little minx keep the diamonds.

The strumpet had already cheated me out of five hundred smackers on the bloody billets-doux and I was damned if she was going to keep the sparklers. So I did what any heartbroken ex-lover would do – I went round the next day while she was out performing at a matinee and turned the place upside down.

Scene Eleven

(We see him frantically searching for the diamonds, through drawers filled with stockings and camisoles, scarves and hand bags.)

CAD. Where are you, dammit?

*(We her a door open and **GERTIE** entering.)*

(Panicking.) Dammit!

(He hides under chaise longue.)

GERTIE. Is that you under the bed, Edward?

CAD. No.

GERTIE. I think it is

CAD. Yes. I'm looking for a cufflink…and I've found it! It's here, on my cuff! But more to the point, what are you doing here? No matinee then?

GERTIE. Lottie filled in for me. You remember her?

CAD. Er…

GERTIE. I thought you'd be back.

CAD. The truth is, I couldn't bear to leave you like that.

GERTIE. In possession of the diamonds.

CAD. They're mine, for God's Sake!

GERTIE. Not any more. I knew you'd come looking for them. Your friend Lord Plaistow did the same to me last year. I wasn't going to be caught twice. They're now safely tucked up in a safety deposit box in Coutts on the Strand.

CAD. Damn your lack of trust and damn Plaistow! What sort of a friend is he? He didn't even warn me what you'd be like!

(To audience.) There was only one solution to this sorry affair. To demand from Lord Plaistow that he pay half of my losses regarding the diamonds. A thoroughly reasonable request. And do you know what? He laughed and told me I could jolly well lump it! I told him I would never forget it.

Scene Twelve

(Back in the present. **MISS APPLEBY** *has returned.)*

CAD. *(To* **MISS APPLEBY**.*)* And I *haven't* forgotten it. Lord Plaistow treated me abominably!

*(***CAD** *is looking over her shoulder as she types.)*

It's spelled 'P L A I S T O W'. Pronounced 'rotter'.

(Enter **MR COLLINS***, carrying boxes of papers.)*

MR COLLINS. Wasn't Lord Plaistow killed in the war?

CAD. Yes, but who wasn't?

MISS APPLEBY. Are you sure this is suitable for publication? You really don't come out of it very well.

CAD. What are you talking about? The point of this tale is quite clearly that I was defeated at the hands of the monstrous regiment of women – because of the inherent unfairness of romantic entanglements.

MISS APPLEBY. What was unfair about it? The diamonds were just a small reward for poor Gertie for putting up with you, keeping you company and goodness knows what else.

CAD. But did I not put up with HER and keep HER company and goodness knows what else? Of course I did! What was my reward? Nothing compared to Gertie's haul.

MISS APPLEBY. What happened to Gertie? I like the sound of her.

CAD. She met a sad and tragic end. She married the Bishop of Norwich.

MISS APPLEBY. Lucky old Bishop!

CAD. My readers need only to know the following:

> *(He dictates to **MISS APPLEBY**.)*

'As a footloose and fancy free bachelor, I dazzled the pre-war social scene and being as popular as ever with the fairer sex, I was no stranger to the delights of theatreland.'

> *(**MISS APPLEBY** tears up pages of dictation and types a short sentence.)*

MR COLLINS. So if we're casting a veil over your private life during this period, what else did you do in London?

CAD. Plenty! I got up late, I played cards in the afternoon and in the evening, I went to my clubs...

MR COLLINS. But did you do any *work*?

CAD. For heaven's sake Collins – don't be so boringly middle class. We were the last glorious flickerings of the gay flaneurs and swaggering boulevardiers! My 'job' as a member of the upper classes was to give ordinary people something to aspire to. To set a standard of elegant behaviour that would encourage them out of their dingy lives to believe they too could enjoy a better, more colourful existence. Everything I did was for them. But that sadly was all about to change.

> *(**MR COLLINS** and **MISS APPLEBY** are open-mouthed. He actually believes this stuff!)*

That gilded era was coming to an end.

> *(Ominous music swells.)*

And so we must come to the Great War.

What is there to say about the war which has not been said already by the likes of Sassoon, Graves, Remarque and all the rest of them?

MISS APPLEBY. What more indeed?

CAD. But history demands that I record my own personal contribution to the allied cause. It was a stepping stone in my journey across the torrential river of life. As soon as war broke out my intimate circle of friends held a meeting in my rooms in the Albany.

Scene Thirteen

(Flashback. We hear a champagne cork pop as **GERALD CHIPPENHAM** *[actor playing* **MR COLLINS***] enters with fizz.)*

CHIPPENHAM. Well this is all jolly exciting!

(Action freezes as **CAD** *addresses audience.)*

CAD. *(To audience.)* Gerald Chippenham was there, along with Walsh-Aynscot, Hudson, Forbes, and van Suidam, and Duncatton. And many others from that youthful elite whose names I have long forgotten. Most of them are dead anyway.

(Action continues.)

CHIPPENHAM. Cavalry or infantry, Foxy?

(Enter **WALSH-AYNSCOT** *[played by actress playing* **MISS APPLEBY***].)*

WALSH-AYNSCOT. Definitely cavalry!

CAD. *(To audience.)* Definitely *neither* if possible! But before I could protest...

CHIPPENHAM. So we're agreed – we all apply for commissions in the cavalry.

WALSH-AYNSCOT. Hussars, I say!

CHIPPENHAM. The dress uniform's a winner

WALSH-AYNSCOT. Damn fine polo team!

CAD. *(To audience.)* They had clearly lost their heads, swept off their feet by that silly poster of Lord Kitchener with his ridiculous moustache and fat forefinger outstretched saying 'Your King and Country Need You.'

(To **FRIENDS.***)* Our King and Country need us...

ALL. Hear hear! Good old Foxy.

CAD. But we are, remember, the officer class. Are we cannon fodder? ARE WE CANNON FODDER? No! We are not! It is the common people whose destiny is to die, as sadly they've always died, in ditches.

CHIPPENHAM. What exactly are you saying?

CAD. That we are the brains of the land. Men like us are able to serve our country far better in administrative posts rather than on the battlefield.

(Stunned silence.)

CHIPPENHAM. Poor show Fox-Ingleby!

*(Actor playing **HUDSON** is now **FORBES**, with a different hat or moustache.)*

FORBES. Give him a white feather!

CAD. *(To audience.)* That was Pat Forbes – not a bad fellow, but not a gentleman. He owed me £30 when he was killed at Loos – and his executors refused to pay up. It was a most unsavoury business.

*(To **FORBES**.)* Steady on, Forbes. I'm just saying, where was Napoleon at Austerlitz? In the front line dodging cannonballs? No, he was behind, organising victory.

CHIPPENHAM. Your point is?

CAD. I am merely suggesting that the really patriotic gesture would be for us all to join up at once...

FORBES. That's more like it!

CAD. ...With the Imperial Supply and Procurement Services Department for the newly formed Ministry of War.

CHIPPENHAM. Nonsense Foxy!

FORBES. He's pulling our leg!

CAD. Any fool can stand in the way of a machine gun bullet – but not everyone can supply a fighting division with hay for its horses or marmalade for its breakfast.

CHIPPENHAM. Very funny, Foxy, but we are all agreed, are we not – the cavalry!

FORBES. The cavalry!

HUDSON. The cavalry!

> *(They **ALL** raise a glass of champagne.)*

CAD. *(Very unconvincingly.)* The cavalry! To the Light Brigade! Or the Heavy one! Whichever Brigade, hurrah!

(To audience.) It was the first defeat of the war, and one that I was at a loss how to reverse. But then a voice from my ancestral past called to me over the years.

> *(We hear an **ELDERLY WOMAN**'s voice barking at him.)*

GRANNY INGLEBY. Edward? Edward?

Scene Fourteen

*(We now see old **GRANNY INGLEBY** – a bad-tempered and bitter old woman in a wheel chair.)*

CAD. *(To audience.)* It was old Granny Ingleby, and I was always her favourite.

GRANNY INGLEBY. Come here young Edward!

*(**YOUNGER CAD** goes over eagerly to sit at her feet. She whacks him round the ear.)*

CAD. Ow! What's that for?

GRANNY INGLEBY. For the good of your health! Your father's too pathetic to bring you up properly so *I'll* have to do it – or you will never turn out to be a great man like your Grandfather. Have I told you about how your Gradfather Jedediah became a war hero when the Prussians laid siege to Paris?

CAD. Yes you have Granny

*(**GRANNY INGLEBY** whacks him round the head again.)*

GRANNY INGLEBY. You'd better learn to lie boy or you are going to get nowhere in this world.

CAD. No Granny I have never heard that story. Please tell it to me...

*(**GRANNY INGLEBY** chuckles. **CAD** listens intently at her feet.)*

Was he a soldier Granny?

(She hits him again.)

GRANNY INGLEBY. Don't be stupid! No he helped the poor starving French.

CAD. And how did he do that?

GRANNY INGLEBY. Rats. Yes, He sold the Frenchies rats to eat.

CAD. Gosh!

GRANNY INGLEBY. Eight francs for a lovely, top quality, pot-ready rodent! Your grandfather made a fortune out of that siege – and never risked his life once! A true hero.

CAD. *(To* **GRANNY INGLEBY.***)* You could say, Granny, it was a 'rats to riches story.'

   *(***GRANNY INGLEBY** *hits him again.)*

Ow!

GRANNY INGLEBY. Shut up, boy and always, ALWAYS remember this…

   *(***CAD** *looks up expectantly. Dramatic pause.)*

No, it's gone.

   *(***GRANNY INGLEBY** *wheels herself away.)*

CAD. *(To audience.)* What an instructive tale. Ingenuity, Fortitude and Profit. What an example to his descendants…

   *(***GRANNY INGLEBY** *fades.)*

(To audience.) And then I suddenly had a brilliant idea! Supplies! Animals… not Rats, but horses! Eureka! Cavalry need horses. Horses become casualties. *Remounts* are necessary. By joining the Remount Department, I'm sort of de facto *in* the cavalry, saving face with the chaps while safely riding a desk!

   *(***CAD** *looks admiringly at himself in the mirror.)*

CAD. Edward, you are a genius! Getting in on the dead equine market! One of the first chaps in history to successfully flog a dead horse! Granny Ingleby would be proud of me!

(To audience.) So without further ado I hopped on a train to see Lord Oldham, the Lord Lieutenant of the County – and coincidentally brother-in-law of the Inspector General of Cavalry.

Scene Fifteen

(**LORD OLDHAM/MR COLLINS** *pops up on the other side of the stage.*)

LORD OLDHAM. Ah, Fox-Ingleby. Yes, I know just the job for you, young man. A cavalry regiment.

CAD. Splendid!

LORD OLDHAM. A cavalry regiment. Leaving on the first boat...to France! Glad to help you to a commission. God speed!

CAD. *(To audience.)* Noooooooooooo! Not so splendid!

   (Beat.)

After that, I'm afraid to say, the meeting went downhill. I suggested that if I were *not* to be charging straight at Fritz's guns with an ornamental sabre, I could perhaps be in charge of the Remount Department.

(To **LORD OLDHAM.***)* ...then you Sir might be the beneficiary of sales of your own fine horses to the cavalry without any veterinary examination and at an advantageous price.

(To audience.) This sensible logistical suggestion was sadly taken the wrong way.

LORD OLDHAM. *(Splenetic.)* By God Sir! Are you attempting to *bribe* me?!

CAD. *(To* **LORD OLDHAM.***)* Bribe you? *Bribe* you? How could you possibly accuse me of such a thing, my Lord? Nothing could be further from the truth! My sole motive is zeal to secure as many of the famous Oldham horses for the service of the country. My reference to the price was simply to record my conviction that £70 is a ludicrously small sum to offer for such magnificent creatures!

LORD OLDHAM. Is that so?

CAD. Absolutely! I can't believe that my sincere and genuine offer has been somehow misunderstood and twisted into such an ugly insinuation.

LORD OLDHAM. For the sake of your father, who I greatly admired, I will accept your word on the matter. I can make no promises, but I will see what I can do.

CAD. You stupid pompous old goat!

(To audience.) ...was what I didn't say.

Thank you, your Lordship.

(To audience.) ...was what I did. I repaired to Grantly Manor to await my new appointment. To my surprise I was met not by William Bedford, but by his wife.

Scene Sixteen

>(**MRS BEDFORD** *enters, bearing a vase of flowers for the drawing room.*)

MRS BEDFORD. I thought you would appreciate something to brighten the place up Sir.

>(*She proceeds to arrange the flowers.*)

CAD. It is Mr Bedford that I need to see.

MRS BEDFORD. I'm afraid William is not here Sir.

CAD. Well that's damned inconvenient. I understand that eight of my staff have already joined up, without so much as a by your leave from their employer. You are to tell William to strike their names off the register of servants.

MRS BEDFORD. *(Cheerily.)* I will do no such thing Sir.

CAD. Have you taken leave of your senses Mrs Bedford?

MRS BEDFORD. *(Genially.)* Not that I know of.

CAD. Then tell William that the men are not to be reinstated.

MRS BEDFORD. I will not. And he will not.

CAD. After thirty-five years' service, I would hate to have to dispense with your husband's services.

MRS BEDFORD. *(Cheerily.)* He's leaving anyway. He's got a Government job.

CAD. What? At his age?

MRS BEDFORD. Yes, it's a job that no decent youngster wants as it doesn't mean any fighting.

CAD. What job?

MRS BEDFORD. He's going to be Remount Officer for Midhamptonshire.

CAD. *(To audience.)* Aaaaargh!!!

> *(***MRS BEDFORD** *leaves and* **CAD** *vents his fury on the vase of flowers, decimating the arrangement. Eventually he composes himself.)*

(To audience.) It is a mark of strength of character that in the face of adversity one does not shy away from tribulations but instead one walks into the fear. The Fox-Inglebys had always been resourceful. Now was another opportunity to display the steely backbone of pragmatism that they displayed throughout the Civil War.

Scene Seventeen

(Back to the present. **MR COLLINS** *enters with a large history book.* **MISS APPLEBY** *resumes her place as stenographer.)*

MR COLLINS. The Civil War, yes. When a Sir Roger Ingleby fought with the Royalists, then joined Cromwell, then rejoined the Cavaliers before becoming a Roundhead again, finally declaring himself a lifelong admirer of Charles II?

CAD. He was no doubt justifiably concerned to be on the right side of history. As indeed am I.

MR COLLINS. The winning side.

CAD. It's certainly preferable to the alternative. I find that if one wants to *write* history, it is advisable to *survive* history.

(Thinks.)

That's rather good. I shall use that in my foreword.

MISS APPLEBY. Usually memoirs have forewords written by admirers.

CAD. Are you offering?

MISS APPLEBY. Certainly not!

CAD. Then if not a foreword, perhaps a cup of tea?

*(***MISS APPLEBY** *exits, annoyed.)*

(Action freezes to address audience.)

I will write the foreword. No-one is a greater admirer of myself than *me*. Anyway, survival in the war was paramount – and I did survive thanks, ironically, to that old scoundrel Bedford betraying, and then abandoning me.

(Back to real time.)

CAD. The young men on my estate had quite rightly joined up, leaving Grantly Manor deserted and destitute. And the authorities asked me – no begged me – no, pretty much put a gun to my head – saying that however reluctant I was, I had to stay behind and manage the estates.

*(**CAD** is pathetically relieved.)*

Yes! Thank God! Saved!

(Composes himself.)

So I did my duty, and took up work of National Importance on the Home Front.

MR COLLINS. *(Sarcastically.)* Good for you!

CAD. I had vital tasks to carry out – such as recruiting, organizing fetes for the Red Cross and patriotic sing-songs with stars from the music-hall. Soldiers might – and probably *did* perform feats of great valour in the field of battle. But where would they be if they were not supported by recruits and medical supplies and a confident civil population?

Scene Eighteen

(Flashback. Bunting appears and a tombola. He spins the wheel and pulls out a ticket. Tea dance music plays.)

CAD. And the winner of the Socks For Soldiers raffle is... Miss Felicity Trowbridge. Number 137

*(A young lady in a fancy hat, **FELICITY**, played by actor playing **MISS APPLEBY**, comes up to claim her prize.)*

FELICITY. But my number is 74.

CAD. So it is. My mistake. Too late to change it. You win.

(He throws away wrong ticket, as he's clearly cheated.)

Your prize. It's dinner – with me!

(He takes her arm and they start to dance.)

I congratulate you on so generously supporting such a vital cause as Footwear for Flanders.

FELICITY. One can't help but admire those who have nobly put themselves in the face of danger for their country.

CAD. Yes, but there are those admirable fellows who prefer to put civic duty before reckless jingoism. Any chump can wangle a commission in some twopenny-halfpenny line regiment and get himself blown up.

FELICITY. *(Dreamily.)* And then of course there are the uniforms...

CAD. You're surely far too sensible a young woman to be put into a state of hysterical ecstasy by the appearance of an ill-fitting khaki uniform of particularly revolting material.

FELICITY. *(Even more dreamily.)* ...and as for the medals...

> *(They continue dancing as* **CAD** *addresses the audience.)*

CAD. *(To audience.)* Whoever had the idea of bestowing medals on so-called heroes deserved to be shot at dawn. Damn that Military Cross! The sight of it made me sick.

(To **FELICITY**.*)* But my dear Felicity, is a husband with a Military Cross and one leg better than a husband with two legs and no medals?

FELICITY. Oh yes!

CAD. *(To audience.)* Of course he isn't – he's incomparably worse! Yet for some incomprehensible reason womenfolk in 1914 were lured by the shiny self-advertising medallion.

(To **FELICITY**.*)* My sweet girl, I'm sure that an M.C. – or whatever the thing is called – is very decorative and glamorous. But is it worth more than, say, an O.B.E. for services to Land Management in the Domestic Economy?

FELICITY. Most definitely!

> *(***FELICITY** *pushes him away, leaving him alone on the dance floor. The music stops suddenly...)*

CAD. *(To audience.)* Damn! There was nothing for it. I had to join the Army.

> *(We hear a bugle play and a drum roll as* **CAD** *changes out of his tweeds and into an army uniform. He looks admiringly at himself in the mirror.)*

(To audience.) There was no doubt that big polished boots, spurs, yellow breeches, a perfectly set tunic

complete with fine red tabs, shiny brass buttons, epaulettes with pips, a big leather belt, yellow tie, gloves, cane – and a hat pulled rakishly down over one eye – all put me in a position to compete with a Military Cross.

(He blows a kiss at himself in the mirror.)

You handsome devil! Khaki suits you!

*(**FELICITY** re-appears and swoons.)*

FELICITY. Edward, I am soooo proud of you.

CAD. Dinner, dance…nightcap in my chambers?

> *(**FELICITY** kisses him and they both dance off to the sound of a jaunty version of "Keep the Home Fires Burning." Flashback ends.)*

Scene Nineteen

(Back in the present. **MR COLLINS** *appears, on the phone.)*

MR COLLINS. So just to clarify when he says he joined the army he actually became a staff officer. Yes, thank you that makes sense. I remember the staff officers... the red-tab brigade... we didn't see much of them at the sharp end did we? ...And he was immediately seconded to the Ministry of National Economy...in Whitehall... so not very near France then... Well thank you for your help Archie, I will try and get a thanks to the Records Office into the acknowledgements...

*(***MISS APPLEBY*** appears.)*

MISS APPLEBY. Good luck with that. I think the only person he is going to thank is himself.

MR COLLINS. You may be right.

MISS APPLEBY. How are you finding the research?

MR COLLINS. Illusory. There is one question that continues to baffle me. Perhaps *you* can help.

MISS APPLEBY. Me? What?

MR COLLINS. Why?

MISS APPLEBY. Why what?

MR COLLINS. *Why* do these women fall for him? What do they see in such a vainglorious charlatan? Perhaps as a representative of the fairer sex can you explain the total...*unfairness* of his success?

*(***MISS APPLEBY*** laughs.)*

MISS APPLEBY. You are not jealous of him are you?

MR COLLINS. Jealous? Me? No, no, no, no, no. Well, Yes. There is no justice...

MISS APPLEBY. He is of course rich...which unfortunately some women like... and he is moderately good looking... if that sort of thing is a contributing factor in your judgements...and he does have a sort of vulnerable quality which appeals to the maternal instincts in some of my gender... and to some impressionable, idealistic types he might seem to be worth saving and might represent a cause to which they could devote themselves...

> (**MR COLLINS** *looks at her very suspiciously as she has a far away look in her eyes...*)

Quite mistakenly of course!

> *(She snaps out of it.)*

> (**CAD** *re-enters wearing coat and hat. He takes them off...*)

CAD. Sorry I'm a trifle late...

MISS APPLEBY. We have been waiting an hour

CAD. Good. I thought it was going to be longer.

I had to see my solicitor as I am suing my tailor. The rascal is deliberately trying to make me look fat. Which is of course why I haven't paid any of his bills. Now where were we?

MISS APPLEBY. We had just got to the bit where you were right and everyone else was wrong.

CAD. Just so. Could you be more specific? Which year precisely was I being right and everyone else was being wrong?

MR COLLINS. 1917 Sir. When you valiantly decided to join up and not to go to the Front.

CAD. Ah yes. My unique abilities were sadly needed by the Ministry Of Supply. But do not for a minute think that life in London was easy. Getting a table at a decent restaurant was difficult. Getting a taxi home was a nightmare! And then there were the air raids!

MISS APPLEBY. Air raids?

CAD. Oh yes! It was an existence of constant trauma, whatever you may have heard.

MR COLLINS. I wouldn't have known, being in Flanders at the time.

CAD. Believe me, death was at our doors. The bomb that fell on the Foyer of the Strand Theatre still makes me shudder to think of it. What if it was in the Stalls? What if I had bought a ticket that night? What if I hadn't been in Brighton at time?

MISS APPLEBY. Why were you in Brighton?

CAD. I had sensibly moved down there when the first air raid warnings began. The ministry needed me too much to risk my life in town.

MR COLLINS. I didn't know that the home front was so hazardous.

CAD. Well now you do. Luckily the Zeppelins eventually threw in the towel and I was able to leave that dreary provincial seaside town and return to civilisation.

> (**CAD** *sits down triumphantly at a desk, laden with piles of paper. He does some signing and stamping of forms. He turns to* **MISS APPLEBY** *who has resumed her position taking down his words.*)

(*To* **MISS APPLEBY**.) But make no mistake. In spite of the satisfactory resolution of all the military challenges confronting me...

> (*He stamps another form.*)

...there there were dark clouds on the horizon. Dark, dark clouds.

> (*Ominous music – "Mars" by Holst. Distant gunfire.*)

MR COLLINS. The German Counter Offensive?

CAD. No, no, no! Much worse.

(Solemnly.) The Counter-Offensive of Cyril Hereward.

MISS APPLEBY. Who?

CAD. Do pay attention, Miss Appleby. Cyril Hereward, if you will remember, was the disagreeable youth who deliberately put his face in the way of my riding crop at Oxford when we were indulging in some harmless tomfoolery involving a bonfire of my tutor's unwanted manuscript. I had quite forgotten him – but sadly he had not forgotten me. But then – who does?

Scene Twenty

> *(Flashback. We see* **CYRIL HEREWARD** *– played by the actor playing* **MR COLLINS**. **HEREWARD** *is the bespectacled young man whom* **CAD** *hit with the riding crop at Oxford. He is in army uniform and has lost an arm. His shadow looms menacingly over* **CAD**. *He signs a letter and hands it offstage. It is placed on* **CAD**'s *desk.)*

CAD. Another damned letter!

> *(He reads it.)*

This one inquiring about my health.

> *(**HEREWARD** dictates the letter. What follows is an exchange of letters.)*

HEREWARD. Could Captain Fox-Ingleby explain if there is any physical or mental disability that prevents him from service with his regiment overseas?

CAD. Last week there was a chit about my date of birth. I was born in the year Mind Your Own Business! Now this.

> *(**CAD** starts to write in reply.)*

Eager though I am to exchange blows with the hated Teuton, my place is on the administrative side. Bayonet thrusters are many. Executive talent is rare.

HEREWARD. You are required to attend a Medical Board on April 7th.

CAD. *(Reading another letter.)* This is outrageous!

> *(He writes another response.)*

I must make it perfectly clear, Sir, that if I am sent off to be uselessly butchered, as if I was of no greater value than anyone else, I am perfectly ready to go. But I demand that I argue my case in person.

HEREWARD. Very well. Come in, Mr Fox-Ingleby.

> (**CAD** *leaves his desk and enters* **HEREWARD**'s *office.*)

CAD. Captain Hereward?

(*To* **HEREWARD**.) You!

HEREWARD. (*Icy politeness.*) Mr Fox-Ingleby, thank you very much for coming in to the War Office.

> (**CAD** *holds out his hand to shake.* **HEREWARD** *can't as he has lost his arm.*)

CAD. (*To audience.*) He had lost his arm in some particularly foolish engagement at the Marne. Now he was using it to make me feel uncomfortable and pursue what was clearly a vendetta against me. And all on account of a silly incident when we were students. Really poor show!

HEREWARD. Please take a seat.

> (**CAD** *sits while* **HEREWARD** *walks round him observing him at close range.*)

You are clearly sound of limb. And by all appearances sound of mind.

CAD. Of course I'm sound of mind. Otherwise I'd be in France!

HEREWARD. So there is *no* reason why you should not be sent to the front?

CAD. (*To audience.*) It was clear that Hereward's persecution of me based on the gratification of a petty revenge would not be abated by reasonable argument. I was in deadly danger. There was not a moment to lose. But what to do?

(**CAD** *gets up, and paces round, perplexed.*)

CAD. I immediately endeavoured to hoist Cyril Hereward by his own petard and have *him* sent back to the front. But due to his damned arm – which he may well have lost on purpose in case of just such an eventuality – he was deemed unfit for action. Quick thinking was required and quick thinking was achieved. I was able to thwart Hereward's advances by making some advances of my own.

(Beat.)

On the wife of *my* superior...

Scene Twenty-One

> (**LADY URSULA CLOPPIN**, *played by actress playing* **MISS APPLEBY**, *appears on the other side of the stage. She is buxom and matronly, but given to passion – particularly for cakes. She is devouring treats from a fancy cake rack.* **CAD** *produces another tray of fancies.*)

CAD. Lady Ursula, if I may be so bold...

LADY URSULA. These really are too good – and you spoil me! One would hardly think that rationing is in place.

CAD. What is the point of being the private secretary of the Chief Under-Secretary of the Ministry of Food if one cannot help one's friends in a time of need.

LADY URSULA. You are a very naughty boy. A lady must consider her figure.

CAD. *(To audience.)* Too late for that.

> (**CAD** *pops another chocolate into* **LADY URSULA**'s *mouth.*)

(To **LADY URSULA**.*)* More of you means more enchantment and delight.

LADY URSULA. Flattery will get you...

CAD. *(To audience.)* Off the hook!

> (**CAD** *kisses her on the neck. She loses herself to passion, pulling off his clothes. Meanwhile* **CAD** *calmly addresses the audience, between kisses.*)

(To audience.) Lady Ursula Cloppin was fat, fifty and lonely. More importantly, she was married to Sir Henry Cloppin, for whom I was temporary private secretary. He was a weak, small, fussy civil servant who spent more time attending to his walrus moustache than his hungry wife. Which was to my advantage.

CAD. *(To* **LADY URSULA.***)* You are my Venus De Milo... my Helen of Troy... my Mona Lisa...

LADY URSULA. *(Moaning.)* Enough of your nonsense!

> *(He pauses.)*

Perhaps a little more...

> *(The kissing continues.)*

CAD. *(To* **LADY URSULA.***)* You are the Eloise to my Abelard... the Cleopatra to my Anthony... the Guinevere to my Lancelot...

LADY URSULA. We must hurry. My husband will be returning from the Ministry presently.

> *(She has had enough of pleasantries and jumps on him.)*

CAD. *(To audience.)* God! I'm being devoured! This must be what it feels like to be a Chelsea bun!

(To **LADY URSULA.***)* Talking of the Ministry, perhaps you could persuade Sir Henry to make my appointment permanent. I would hate you to find I had suddenly been transferred to France.

LADY URSULA. My dear dear boy, I doubt very much if my husband will consider my entreaties...

CAD. I do have access to unlimited sugar and meat coupons.

LADY URSULA. I'll see what I can do.

CAD. Chelsea bun?

> *(He pops a Chelsea bun in her mouth and disentangles himself.)*

Scene Twenty-Two

(**HEREWARD/MR COLLINS** *appears again having summoned* **CAD** *to see him once more. He is reading a letter.*)

HEREWARD. *(Reading.)* Captain Fox-Ingleby has now been deemed an indispensable part of the war effort and can in no circumstances be transferred to active duty at the front. Signed Sir Henry Cloppin, Ministry of War.

>(**CAD** *has now rearranged his clothing and presents himself, standing to attention.*)

CAD. Thank you, Major Hereward. It's a bitter pill to swallow but I know where my duty lies.

HEREWARD. So you are in charge of food coupons! Is that why my sister and her children can't get any?

CAD. I am shocked at such a vile insinuation Major! That suggestion is beneath you...

(To audience.) ...though entirely true. Hereward and his beastly family would find themselves on extremely short rations for the remainder of the war. Still, very healthy diet, I'm told.

HEREWARD. I expect you think you've won, Fox-Ingleby.

CAD. Probably because I *have*, Hereward! Toodle pip!

>*(Flashback ends.)*

Scene Twenty-Three

(Back in present. We see **MISS APPLEBY** *is typing this and stops.)*

CAD. *(Dictating.)* ...so, to cut a long story short I triumphed over jealous rivals by sheer hard work and dedication to the war effort. My contribution to the supply economy was deemed just too essential to risk front line service.

MISS APPLEBY. Bravo!

CAD. You know, Miss Appleby I may appear very confident, but I'm actually very shy. Perhaps that's why these bullies pick on me. The likes of Hereward sensed my innate vulnerability. I just want you to know, that even if I can't talk about it because it was hush hush, I had a good war.

(He is clearly trying to ingratiate himself and gain sympathy. She looks at him less critically.)

MISS APPLEBY. I quite understand. Do you have any other wartime achievements to record for posterity?

CAD. I suppose I *could* mention all these medals I received...

*(***CAD*** produces a framed display of a large number of medals.)*

...but I don't want to appear immodest.

MISS APPLEBY. That wouldn't do.

CAD. This one is the Grand Imperial Order of Smirnoff, First Class...

MISS APPLEBY. And what is it for?

CAD. It is for bravely importing Russian Vodka at the height of the German naval blockade. Talking of which – perhaps you would like to join me for a cocktail?

(He is a little flirty. She is prim and embarrassed.)

MISS APPLEBY. Thank you, but I am attending a poetry reading this evening.

CAD. Poor you. Well I shan't keep you then.

(He dismisses her. She exits. He returns to admiring his own medals.)

*(***MR COLLINS** *reappears.)*

Ah, Collins. For the historical record I think it's probably best if we include ALL my medals, don't you?

MR COLLINS. Do you not feel embarrassed that you won medals in a war in which you did not fire a shot?

CAD. Don't imagine I didn't spend every minute on the Home Front wishing myself in the trenches, firing handguns and throwing stink-bombs or whatever the technical terms were.

MR COLLINS. They were called Mills bombs.

CAD. I am sure they were. I know you were at Passchendaele – you put it on your CV for some reason – but let me assure you that I suffered too. And perhaps history will say that you were the luckier.

MR COLLINS. I doubt it.

(Action freezes as **CAD** *talks to audience.)*

CAD. *(To audience.)* Actually, the comparison holds. Collins may have suffered on the hills and valleys of the battlefield. But I too toiled on the slopes and contours of Lady Ursula.

(Back to **MR COLLINS.***)* It is the truth. Suffice to say I did my duty without complaint and it was with some relief that I heard the bells ring out declaring the armistice. It was over.

Scene Twenty-Four

(Flashback. We hear church bells ringing out. **CAD** *picks up phone.)*

CAD. Lady Ursula? It's over. I mean between us. I am sure you understand. All good things must come to an end including the war. And so we must go our separate ways.

(We see **LADY URSULA** *sobbing down another phone as he holds the receiver away from his ear.)*

Oh, and can you send round my silk pyjamas that I seem to have left in your bedroom?

(More sobs down phone.)

(To audience.) So the armistice came. And in my opinion it did not come a moment too soon. For I was bored with the war. The whole thing had become hysterical. But two tremendous victories had been registered. Britain had defeated the Kaiser.

And I had defeated Major Cyril Hereward.

(Suddenly sombre.)

Of course there were losses too. Terrible losses that one cannot forget. I never did get those pyjamas back.

(Spotlight on **CAD** *in sad moment when curtain comes down.)*

End of Act One

ACT TWO

Scene One

(We see back projection of newspaper headlines 'GENERAL ELECTION CALLED' 'VOTES FOR WOMEN KEY ISSUE' 'CAN MR LLOYD GEORGE WIN?' We are in flashback.)

*(**CAD** sports a big blue rosette. It is election day 1918.)*

RETURNING OFFICER. *(Voice over.)* As the returning officer for the constituency of South East Midhamptonshire, and following a third recount, I declare the votes as follows: William George Morrison (Labour) 1,278. Archibald Gordon Macdonnel (Liberal) 9,378.

*(There are gasps and cheers from the audience. **CAD** looks disconcerted as this is very high.)*

Edward Hercules Fox-Ingleby (Conservative) 9,396.

(More cheers and boos.)

I duly declare that Edward Fox-Ingleby is the Member of Parliament for South East Midhamptonshire.

CAD. Thank you very much indeed. And thank you to all the volunteers who have been canvassing for me – many of them touchingly workers from my own Grantly estate!

(Boos.)

CAD. Thank you to everybody who has worked so hard to make this resounding landslide victory possible.

(Boos.)

Yes, yes, I am sure a few of you are disappointed. But so was I. A very disappointing set of opponents whingeing on about social reform, Trade Unions, the League of Nations and all that claptrap. My own three point manifesto was very simple and very popular. One – Hang the Kaiser...

(Cheers.)

Two – Life pensions for all of us war veterans...

(Cheers.)

Three – Hang the Kaiser!

(Cheers again – everyone's happy.)

(His wife **DIANA** *enters carrying a baby.)*

DIANA. Congratulations Darling.

(Camera pops; they pose for happy family photos.)

CAD. *(To audience.)* Did I mention I had got married? Silly of me. Must have slipped my mind. Anyway the selection committee were very clear on the matter. No single gentlemen were allowed to stand for a Tory seat even if they did bat for the right side. Which I jolly well do – whatever nonsense you may have read about life at dear old Eton. So married I became – to the lovely Diana. Diana was, of course, beautiful, dutiful, obedient – and the daughter of an Earl. And very soon she was also mother to my child. Er...

DIANA. Anne.

CAD. *(To audience.)* Yes. I wanted to call her Ursula as a tribute to my recent benefactress and to appease her wrath – but Diana wasn't having any of it for some reason. So Anne it was. Like all babies she looked like a raw beetroot and was healthy and fat. Ursula would indeed have been a better name. Still, there I was with my perfect family – and I was a perfect family man.

*(**CAD** kisses his wife goodbye.)*

*(To **DIANA**.)* Sorry darling I'm going to be in town for a few days. The House is sitting late and there's important government business to attend to. The Prime Minister is insisting I be there.

*(**CAD** sighs unconvincingly.)*

(To audience.) And it's true – I was busy. Familiarising myself with the workings of Westminster and sucking up to the incompetents who ran the country. First of all I had the responsibility of making my maiden speech.

Scene Two

(Light changes. **CAD** *is in House of Commons.)*

CAD. Mr Speaker, as is traditional I would like to pay tribute to my predecessor Sir Edward Knighton-Berry who did such an excellent job for his constituents for many years.

(Sounds of 'Hear Hear!')

(To audience.) The old booby had hung onto the seat for far too long when there were much better and younger men waiting in the wings.

One of them, namely myself, lived locally and was therefore an ideal candidate who wouldn't have to waste time pretending to be interested in some godawful constituency in the middle of nowhere like urgh... Reading!

*(***CAD*** back addressing the House of Commons.)*

I am sure Sir Edward would have been proud of my achievement in winning this challenging safe seat – and now I can set about the realistic work of responsible government. And my two priorities are... One: to stop the ludicrously impractical idea of trying to hang the Kaiser. And two: put an end to the ridiculously uneconomic idea of providing pensions for all veterans.

(There are cheers and boos.)

Scene Three

(Lighting change – we are back in the present with **MR COLLINS***, writing his autobiography.)*

MR COLLINS. But how on earth did you get the seat?

CAD. I went to Eton. And then I went to Oxford.

MR COLLINS. I meant that if Sir Edward was by all accounts so popular, how exactly did you get selected?

CAD. That's an interesting story. I think the Party recognised the abilities of a younger more progressive man with a distinguished war record who was more in touch with modern politics than the admirable though antiquated provincial knight.

MR COLLINS. And that was you...

CAD. Obviously.

(To audience.) Besides, the senile old nincompoop was a menace to the party. He advocated the so-called rights of the Trade Unions, sat on administrative boards to help rural workers and ingratiated himself with the working classes.

(To **MR COLLINS**.*)* Poor Sir Edward was from a different generation and had neglected one influential group of potential voters. Women. It was the duty of some public spirited citizen to point this out.

Scene Four

(We are in flashback – how the **CAD** *got selected for the seat. A young actress,* **FLORENCE**, *enters. She is played by the actress playing* **MISS APPLEBY**. **CAD** *sits down to interview her.)*

CAD. So, Miss Waddley – or may I call you Florence?

FLORENCE. Of course Sir.

CAD. Florence. You were excellent playing the maid in 'Mrs Gadsby's Confession'.

FLORENCE. Thank you kindly sir.

CAD. But I now have a more interesting role for you. I want you to play the part of a furious young suffragette who has been cruelly denied the vote by a silly old conservative fool.

FLORENCE. And what is the play called Sir?

CAD. It's an experimental piece which sets out to challenge the audience and make them question what is reality.

FLORENCE. I am more of a music hall artiste to be honest. I have ambitions to play more serious roles, but I would prefer to establish myself as a character actress in light comedies.

CAD. This role will be funny, I promise.

*(***FLORENCE*** is still unsure.)*

And it will be exceedingly well remunerated.

FLORENCE. When do I start?

(Still in flashback, we cut to **SIR KNIGHTON-BERRY** *making a speech. He is very old fashioned, wearing a top hat. A back*

projection shows a poster reading 'Vote For Sir Edward Knighton-Berry'. **SIR KNIGHTON-BERRY** *is played by the actor playing* **MR COLLINS**.*)*

Scene Five

KNIGHTON-BERRY. As your Member of Parliament I of course support the reform of the Insurance Act which answers a great need in our...

FLORENCE. What about votes for women?

KNIGHTON-BERRY. My dear Lady we have given votes to women.

FLORENCE. Only those over thirty. What about the rest of us who did all the work in the war?

KNIGHTON-BERRY. I am afraid that Parliament decided that young women are too impressionable to be allowed to...

FLORENCE. I am not impressed by you!!

(Laughter and boos.)

KNIGHTON-BERRY. Madam I am afraid this is exactly my point, a refusal to engage in reasonable debate...

FLORENCE. Free half the human race!

(She throws assorted vegetables at him which he dodges.)

KNIGHTON-BERRY. Really, Madam please desist or I will call the constabulary

FLORENCE. We are not law breakers – we want to be law makers!

(She rushes up to him and tries to grab his notes.)

KNIGHTON-BERRY. Unhand me Madam

(They have a struggle and emerge with her handcuffed to him.)

FLORENCE. Equality for all! Embrace the Struggle!

(She raises her arms and like a puppet he has to follow her movements.)

Victory for Justice!

(More cheers and boos.)

CAD. *(To audience.)* She really is awfully good. Worth every penny.

*(**CAD** then addresses the crowd offstage.)*

I say everyone, this is a poor show. I mean Sir Knighton-Berry is a very old man. He's nearly sixty for heaven's sake.

*(**KNIGHTON-BERRY** is now struggling and collapses under the strain.)*

FLORENCE. Lawks! He's having a seizure! Someone call a doctor!

(She helps him off the stage still handcuffed.)

CAD. *(Calling offstage.)* Yes, someone call a doctor for this very sick and very old man!

(To audience.) I don't consider myself in any way to blame for Knighton Berry's unfortunate collapse and retirement on the grounds of ill health. At his age it was irresponsible to attempt to appear in public with obviously underlying medical issues.

Scene Six

(Back in the present with the **MR COLLINS**.*)*

CAD. The activities of Miss Florence Waddley merely triggered the inevitable. And she sadly went to jail as an early martyr for female emancipation. But in the meantime there was an election to be fought – and indeed won – by a new champion of the women's cause.

MR COLLINS. Yourself.

CAD. The very same.

MR COLLINS. But up to this point your opinions on women's suffrage were the exact opposite of the position you now adopted.

CAD. It's called Politics. Leadership. Vision. It is why my parliamentary career blossomed and I increased my majority in the 1922 election. No mean feat in a period of political instability and coalition.

*(***MR COLLINS** *produces copy of Hansard.)*

MR COLLINS. To be honest I am having some difficulty keeping track of your political views during this period. Because initially you supported Lloyd George and the Coalition.

CAD. He was the Great Leader, The Welsh Wizard, the man who won the war and who promised me an Under-secretary's post.

MR COLLINS. Which he didn't give you.

CAD. No, but that had no part in my decision to desert the Welsh Windbag and his sinking coalition and pledge my allegiance to the future in the form of Mr Bonar Law. It was a painful decision but one taken entirely on principle. If I have a fault it is that I have always put my principles above self-interest.

*(**MR COLLINS** reading from Hansard.)*

MR COLLINS. Your old friend Freddy Duncatton, the MP for Reading, called you to account when you changed sides.

Scene Seven

(We are in flashback in the House of Commons. **DUNCATTON** *is played by actor playing* **MR COLLINS**.*)*

CAD. The coalition is dead. Can any intelligent member continue to give his allegiance to a rotting corpse which is lying upon a mortuary slab underneath a sheet? Can a realist worship a ghost? Of course not. Which is why I have decided to commit myself to a live, vital, resilient conservatism as personified by the very brilliant and Right Honourable Member for Glasgow Central, Mr Andrew Bonar Law.

DUNCATTON. Judas!

CAD. *(To audience.)* To which I responded with my customary spontaneous wit...

> *(***CAD*** in the Commons clearly has no idea how to respond...)*

You sir are a...er...a...well er...

DUNCATTON. What?

CAD. A...complete...and utter...er...Ass!!!

> *(Murmurs of disapproval.)*

SPEAKER. *(Voice offstage.)* Order! Order!

Scene Eight

(Back in the present with **MISS APPLEBY**.*)*

CAD. *(To* **MISS APPLEBY**.*)* Not only did I squish Duncatton like an annoying wasp at a picnic with my rapier-like riposte, but having called me 'Judas' I had no other option but to report him to the Speaker for Blasphemy – and had him suspended from the House.

MISS APPLEBY. That's very tough.

CAD. Yes, it was – for me. He was one of my oldest friends. But one must be charitable, and it probably wasn't Duncatton's fault he'd blown a gasket. During the war Freddy had transferred from the Hussars to a line regiment to see more action and got himself bombed senseless.

> *(***MR COLLINS*** re-enters with copies of Hansard.)*

Shell shock accounted for many strange actions in those days, as we who had been through the hell of air raids could testify.

MR COLLINS. Really?

CAD. Yes. I forgave Duncatton even when he called me a 'snivelling shirker' in the Tea Room. Of course, I had to have him deselected from the party and pour a pot of tea on his head. But my sympathies were entirely with him.

MR COLLINS. So have I got this right? You switched from Lloyd George to back Bonar Law and you then transferred your allegiance to Mr Baldwin...

CAD. A great man who recognised my talents and gave me my first ministerial job.

MR COLLINS. Though you called him an idiot for calling a snap General election in 1923 which he then lost badly to the Labour Party.

(We see headline 'BALDWIN CALLED AN IDIOT BY FOX-INGLEBY MP'.)

CAD. I never called him an idiot. And if I did it was strictly off the record and not meant to be repeated. And shame on whoever did.

MR COLLINS. It is recorded in Hansard.

CAD. One mustn't trust everything that appears in print, Mr Collins. Mr Baldwin's error of judgement was salvaged a year later by my friends at the *Daily Mail* who revealed that the Labour party was in cahoots with the Russian Communists.

MR COLLINS. Oh yes, the infamous Zinoviev letter...

MISS APPLEBY. Wasn't it subsequently found to be a forgery?

CAD. Yes, but it *felt* true and certainly the public thought it *was* true and as I argued at the time, it probably *was* true even if technically it *wasn't*.

MISS APPLEBY. I'm surprised anyone was taken in by it.

MR COLLINS. *(Sarcastically.)* It was *somewhat* convenient that four days before the general election, a Tory newspaper discovered a letter directly linking the Labour party with the worldwide Bolshevik revolution.

MISS APPLEBY. Who would have thought it?

(They both laugh.)

CAD. That is incredibly cynical of both of you. The important thing for Britain – and here the *Daily Mail* was absolutely right – was that the Labour party was, and is, full of bolshies and pinkos and other undesirables and needed to be booted out accordingly. We won and they lost. Yah boo!

(He sits down triumphantly and pours himself a large drink.)

MR COLLINS. But that's not the only story the papers were interested in, was it?

CAD. What do you mean?

MR COLLINS. I hate to bring this up, but throughout this period you were regularly featured in the gossip columns.

CAD. I don't think anyone is interested in my private life.

MISS APPLEBY. I think they are. And I don't think an autobiography can focus only on weighty matters of state.

CAD. So you would rather I dwelt on the mysteries of the human heart?

MISS APPLEBY. If this is going to be a frank and honest account of your life.

CAD. Well, honesty is my middle name.

MR COLLINS. I thought it was Hercules. Though at various points you have called yourself Hotspur, Galahad and Alexander.

CAD. Don't be so pedantic, Collins it does you no favours. As I was saying, I was a wealthy, influential, highly respected and happily married man with an adoring wife and a beautiful daughter...

MR COLLINS. Anne?

CAD. Well remembered. But no matter how hard I tried to be a good father and a loyal husband...

(To audience.) ...and I did try...for *months*...

(To **MR COLLINS** *and* **MISS APPLEBY**.*)* ...it was inevitable that like so many great men before me, temptation should be put in my path.

MISS APPLEBY. So you're going to say that it's the women who are to blame?

CAD. Not at all. I would be the first to admit that I am not a saint. But it's important to understand there are two sides to every story...

(To audience.) ...and this book is going to tell MY side.

(To **MISS APPLEBY.***)* However much I fought against it, I was ultimately weak in the face of overwhelming feminine charms. I'm sorry if you find that disappointing, but I am at heart a simple man and only flesh and blood.

MR COLLINS. Will you excuse me, suddenly I feel a little nauseous.

*(***MR COLLINS** *exits.)*

MISS APPLEBY. I had better check he's all right.

*(***MISS APPLEBY** *exits.)*

CAD. *(To audience.)* In a sense they were right. Times had changed and I had to behave differently. I had put the days of impoverished mistresses in Maida Vale behind me.

(Beat.)

My *new* mistress was rich – and from New York. Violetta was five foot eight, with square shoulders and a full bosom. None of your modern flat-chested flapper foolery about her! Her dazzlingly white skin was offset by a pair of black, deep-set eyes. She was the perfect embodiment of American womanhood.

Scene Nine

> *(We go into flashback. Enter* **VIOLETTA**, *a sassy American, smoking a cigarette and blowing smoke in his face.* **VIOLETTA** *is played by actress playing* **MISS APPLEBY**. *We hear jazz music playing as she comes up and kisses the* **CAD**.*)*

> *(**VIOLETTA** finally speaks. She has a grating, whiny New York voice.)*

VIOLETTA. Oh my! Mr Fox-Ingleby you are one hell of a funny guy! And so well read! Winslow! Get in here Winslow! You gotta hear this Fox-Ingleby guy!

> *(Enter* **WINSLOW BUDDINGTON STARRET** *[played by* **MR COLLINS***], a boring financier.)*

CAD. *(To audience.)* Winslow Buddington Starret was a very wealthy New York stockbroker. You could smoke two whole cigars while he told you about the purchasing power of the Indian rupee.

WINSLOW. I gotta tell you, Edward, the future is loans. That's where the smart money is. Liberty loans, War loans, Victory loans... Wall Street was slow on the uptake but loans aren't debts, Edward. Oh no! Don't make that mistake. No sirree. My firm was in early and bought big. It's like buying a pizza – you know what a pizza is Edward?

> *(While* **WINSLOW** *bores on,* **CAD** *and* **VIOLETTA** *are canoodling and have left the room.* **WINSLOW** *carries on to no-one.)*

It's an Italian flatbread with a tomato and cheese topping, but that's not the point. The point is the financial analogy – and this is where it gets interesting. The bigger the pizza the bigger your slice. Then you add in the extra toppings and your share is significantly larger than the... Edward? Edward?

> *(**CAD** and **VIOLETTA** return somewhat dishevelled.)*

CAD. That's fascinating, Winslow.

VIOLETTA. *(Very bored.)* Isn't it just?

CAD. *(To audience.)* Like the wives of almost all rich Americans, Violetta was monumentally bored with her husband's conversation, his face and his lovemaking. Fortunately like almost all rich American men, his attempts at the latter were intermittent and unsuccessful. Winslow never stood a chance against the charms of a Fox-Ingleby.

> *(He admires himself in the mirror again.* **WINSLOW** *slaps* **CAD** *on back.)*

WINSLOW. Great to meet you Edward, and thanks for looking after the little lady. You're a gentleman.

CAD. Oh yes.

(To audience.) And what should a gentleman do in the circumstances? I did the only decent thing – I hired the flabby faced drone to handle my financial interests and took on his wife to handle my amorous interests. Everything was as the Americans would say 'tickety-boo'.

Scene Ten

(Back in the present **CAD** *is continuing to dictate to* **MISS APPLEBY**. **MR COLLINS** *re-enters.)*

CAD. Are you fully recovered, Mr Collins?

MR COLLINS. It must be something I ate.

CAD. I was concluding that all that needs to be said on the matter of my marriage is that situation was 'complicated' and a source of some regrettable unhappiness.

(He looks tearful. **MR COLLINS** *exits again, looking sick.)*

MR COLLINS. Sorry!

*(***CAD*** then brightens immediately.)*

CAD. But more importantly my public life was beginning to take off, as I was widely spoken of as a rising star in the world of politics.

(We see on the back projection the Evening Sketch *newspaper with headline 'FOX-INGLEBY GIVEN MINOR POST'.)*

MISS APPLEBY. You were appointed Deputy Parliamentary Under-Secretary for the Ministry of Fine Arts?

CAD. It was a new ministry, so obviously those in charge had to be Old Etonians. But lest you should think my life was a bed of roses there was a worm lurking in my Garden of Eden. And that worm was a rat. A sewer rat from Fleet Street employing yellow journalism to bring down the noblest of public servants due to their serpentine bitterness and envy.

MISS APPLEBY. So is that a worm, a rat or a snake?

CAD. All three, Miss Appleby. In the interests of accountability I had foolishly agreed to give an interview to one of the rags about my exciting plans for popularising Stonehenge.

Scene Eleven

(We are in flashback. **CAD** *greets journalist who enters.)*

CAD. Please come in Mr...er...

HEREWARD. Hereward.

(It is Cad's one-armed nemesis. His empty sleeve hangs loose by his side.)

CAD. My God! It's you! I can't believe you're a journalist!

HEREWARD. And I can't believe you're a Government Minister, but such are the vagaries of fate. I joined the *Evening Sketch* upon my demobilisation.

CAD. *(To audience.)* At the time I thought to myself, this man was trying to ruin my life – single-handedly. But then I thought 'no'. This was not a joke worthy of a minister of the crown, so I decided to refrain from making it.

(To **HEREWARD**.*)* You're the man who tried to ruin my life – single-handedly!

(To audience.) So I changed my mind. It's not against the law.

HEREWARD. I shall ignore your puerile remark Fox-Ingleby.

CAD. Well let's get on with it. The Stonehenge development plan is modern, progressive and will revolutionise the Stonehenge experience.

HEREWARD. By building a tea room

CAD. Indeed.

HEREWARD. Inside the stone circle?

CAD. And not just a tea room. I envisage druid themed milk bars, Celtic chocolate kiosks and Stone Age soda fountains all surrounded by vast Neolithic car parks for the thousands of visitors.

HEREWARD. It sounds quite ghastly.

CAD. Don't be such a Luddite! Move with the times! This is what the public wants!

HEREWARD. The public also want to know who has been buying up the land surrounding Stonehenge.

CAD. I have no idea.

HEREWARD. I'll tell you. It has been bought by a friend of yours. Toby Bletchworth. And you two are going to split the profits fifty-fifty.

CAD. That is completely untrue.

(*To audience.*) It's seventy-five twenty-five. I'm not a complete idiot!

HEREWARD. And this isn't the first dubious financial deal with which you have been associated.

CAD. Oh really! I don't think the readers of the *Evening Sketch* are interested in reheated tittle-tattle from the past. They want to hear about my radical vision for the City of London – tearing down the sadly empty outdated old churches designed by Wren or whatever his name was – and replacing them with much-needed new banks and insurance companies, embracing modern architecture and looking to the future needs of Britain!

HEREWARD. And do you hold shares by proxy in both the Consolidated Insurance Company and the Amalgamated Imperial Bank?

CAD. Damn your impudence!

How dare you insinuate any form of impropriety on my behalf. This interview is at an end!

*(**CAD** changes into a dinner jacket and bowtie.)*

(To audience.) The disturbing interest of the gutter press in my business affairs was compounded by the disturbing interest of my wife in my extramarital affairs. The matter came to head after a dinner to celebrate my dazzling promotion from Deputy Under-secretary to Under-secretary.

Scene Twelve

(We are still in flashback. **CAD** *and his wife* **DIANA** *are preparing for bed.* **CAD** *removes his shoes as* **DIANA** *removes her make up and jewellery.)*

CAD. Any reason you moped through the entire meal?

DIANA. I'm tired, Edward.

CAD. I am tired too Diana after a long day at the House looking after the nation's affairs. However, you don't see me sulking like a silly school girl, do you?

DIANA. You clearly find it easy to be cheerful when you are sitting next to Violetta.

CAD. What exactly does that mean?

DIANA. Exactly what I said.

CAD. And you imply?

DIANA. Nothing is implied beyond…

CAD. Beyond what?

DIANA. Beyond what is common knowledge.

CAD. *(To audience.)* Crikey! That was a bit of a googly. It had never occurred to me that Diana would hear anything about me and Violetta. I thought I had better bluff it out.

(To **DIANA.***)* I don't know what you mean!

DIANA. I wouldn't have minded so much if you hadn't flaunted it. But the fact that you don't seem to have *tried* to keep it a secret is what is so insulting!

CAD. Of course I tried!

DIANA. So you admit it!

CAD. *(To audience.)* Damn! Tricked into a confession! My tactic of lofty denial was in tatters!

DIANA. I didn't mind so much all the other times, when you were at least a little more concerned about being discovered – but you were spotted checking into a hotel with Violetta in Bury St Edmunds!

CAD. *(To audience.)* Curses! I thought Bury St Edmonds would be safe as one couldn't possibly have any acquaintances in such a ghastly hole. I needed a new tack so I went for righteous indignation which usually does the trick.

*(To **DIANA**.)* You've been spying on me damn you!

DIANA. *And* you were in Ludlow last August with a pretty little blonde. I must say you were doing very well in August. Unfaithful to me and to Violetta at the same time.

CAD. *(To audience.)* I had to concede that was quite clever, so I went all in guns blazing.

*(To **DIANA**.)* So what are you going to do? Divorce me?

DIANA. I am not sure.

CAD. *(To audience.)* This was bad. It sounded like she was serious. Time to turn on the waterworks.

*(**CAD** crumples to his knees weeping.)*

*(To **DIANA**.)* But darling, sweetheart, just think what would happen to my political career if you were to divorce me. Those sanctimonious swine on the local selection committee would have me out of the seat in no time. It would ruin me.

DIANA. Yes I suppose it would.

CAD. And if you cited Violetta think of the scandal for her.

DIANA. *(More cheerful.)* I am...

CAD. *(To audience.)* Panic Stations! How can she be so cool and calm. Violetta's husband is my stockbroker for God's sake. Time to bring in the child.

(To **DIANA**.*)* Think of our daughter... Anne? Yes, Anne. You don't want to bring disgrace on the poor little mite just because her father has had an idle fling or two or three?

DIANA. Leave Anne out of it.

CAD. *(To audience.)* Mmm. Trying to make her guilty about the infant wasn't going to work. Clearly nothing for it but to fall upon her mercy.

(To **DIANA**.*)* Darling, my dear darling Diana! What can I possibly do to make it up to you?

DIANA. Promise not to see that woman again

CAD. The blonde in Ludlow or Violetta?

DIANA. You know who I mean!

CAD. Oh all right, all right I will promise you anything.

(To audience.) Which was true. I will promise anything.

DIANA. Do you love me?

CAD. Of course I do. Mere words cannot express the depth of my love. It is like a bottomless well of...

DIANA. Yes, forget the words. It will have to be actions. You will give up Violetta and never see her again.

CAD. I swear it. I have lapsed and I have let you down. It will not happen again. I have learnt my lesson.

> (**DIANA** *kisses his head as he kneels. Then she leaves.)*

(To audience.) The lesson being – don't get caught. Diana was an angel, but unfortunately Violetta being American was not quite so understanding...

Scene Thirteen

(Still in flashback.)

CAD. Violetta my darling, it breaks my heart, but I think it might be better for all of us if you and I were to go our separate ways...

>*(A shoe is thrown from the wings which he narrowly dodges.)*

VIOLETTA. *(Offstage.)* You lousy scumbag!

>*(Another shoe whizzes past his head, before **VIOLETTA** enters in a rage.)*

You don't dump me buster! I'm gonna tell Winslow about us...and get him HIM to divorce ME citing YOU as my lover! I'm going to ruin YOU forever!

CAD. *(To audience.)* Why does everyone I meet want to ruin me? It's so unfair. I know it's flattering when a woman scorned turns into a fury from hell, but it's no fun, I can assure you.

>*(**VIOLETTA** throws more items to hand at him.)*

VIOLETTA. I'm going to drag your name through the gutter! You'll be finished!

CAD. *(To audience.)* At that moment I found Violetta's charming nose and delightful embonpoint somehow *less* attractive than I had previously.

VIOLETTA. And for the record, lover-boy, you're not half as good in bed as Winslow! And he's a washout!

CAD. *(To audience.)* Now that was a low blow! I thought we had always been honest with each other – but now she was lying. No wonder I had to call it off.

>*(Phone rings.)*

CAD. *(To* **VIOLETTA.***)* Excuse me, I'd better take this. it's probably a matter of national importance. I'm sure you understand.

VIOLETTA. What I understand is that you're a two-faced, two-bit, two-timing punk!

(She storms out. **CAD** *ignores her.)*

CAD. Fox-Ingleby speaking. Ah, yes, Minister.

(Slightly panic-stricken.)

Right. Right away Minister! I understand!

Scene Fourteen

(Still in flashback. Moustachioed **MINISTER** *[played by actor playing* **MR COLLINS***] appears to reprimand* **CAD**.*)*

CAD. *(Breathless.)* Minister, you wanted to see me.

MINISTER. Now look here Fox-Ingleby you're in deep trouble.

CAD. Is this about the misunderstanding involving the sale of the stained glass window in Lincoln Cathedral to the Oklahoma Pet Food Company?

MINISTER. No it isn't.

CAD. If it's about demolishing that Roman villa to make way for a bypass, I can explain...

MINISTER. No, it's about this journalist from the *Evening Sketch* who's sniffing around your wartime record.

CAD. I deny everything! Whatever it is! I swear on the life of my firstborn son that the charges against me are wholly unfounded!

(To audience.) The truth was Hereward was raking up the past and deliberately misinterpreting certain wartime events from which I had inadvertently profited.

Scene Fifteen

(Still in flashback. We see a back-projected wartime headline: 'WESTERN FRONT STALEMATE – MUNITIONS CRISIS LOOMS'.)

*(**CAD** dons deerstalker and is handed a shotgun. He fires at an imaginary bird.)*

CAD. Missed dammit! There's something wrong with this gun.

*(He is joined by an American businessman **OTIS WINCHESTER** [played by **MR COLLINS** actor].)*

OTIS. I was told you were a man who knew about guns. Otis Winchester the Third.

(They shake hands.)

CAD. Edward Fox-Ingleby the three hundred and twentieth. Old family.

(To audience.) It was a perfectly straightforward shooting weekend in 1916 on Buffy Marchant's estate. The usual mix of Government ministers and American businessmen looking for contracts.

*(**OTIS** shoots. Bang! One bird falls down.)*

CAD. I say! Good shot!

OTIS. It's all about having the right equipment. I know, I'm in the munitions business.

CAD. What a coincidence. I've been seconded to the Ministry of Munitions.

OTIS. You don't say!

(Bang! Two birds come down.)

One thing I know is that you don't want to have faulty artillery in the middle of a war.

CAD. No indeed.

OTIS. And I gather that your ministry is about to award a major contract for a million shells for an eighteen pounder gun to the Military Industrial Corporation of East Pennsylvania.

CAD. I couldn't comment on that.

OTIS. Obviously. But I feel it's my duty to tell you that the Military Industrial Corporation is run by an immigrant family with pro-German interests. It would be a great shame if they deliberately produced dud shells for the British Army.

CAD. I can see that. What would you suggest?

OTIS. There is *another* shell manufacturer which is staunchly pro-British.

CAD. Really? And would this be a more reliable alternative to the Military Industrial Corporation?

OTIS. Yes sir. It's the Industrial Military Corporation of West Pennsylvania.

CAD. Run by…yourself?

(Bang! **OTIS** *shoots and loads of birds rain down.)*

OTIS. You're no fool Edward Fox-Ingleby the 320th.

Scene Sixteen

(Return to present. **MISS APPLEBY** *is typing up from his dictation.)*

CAD. *(To* **MISS APPLEBY**.*)* It was my duty to my country and our brave boys on the front to make sure we had the very best ordnance available, and so I made sure the shell contract was changed with immediate effect.

MISS APPLEBY. Is there something I'm missing? I don't see why this is a scandal or why Hereward would consider it so.

CAD. It *wasn't* a scandal. I had done nothing wrong.

(To audience.) Although it was somewhat embarrassing when The Industrial Military Corporation insisted on giving me a large block of shares after the deal went through.

MISS APPLEBY. I still don't follow...

CAD. *(To audience.)* Good! Let's hope no-one else does! I suppose if I was at fault at all, it was in allowing myself to be bullied into accepting the damn shares. But at the time I regarded them not as a personal reward but as a symbol of the joint cooperation between our two great countries that allowed us to win the war. But I had nothing to worry about – Hereward didn't have any solid proof. All Old Foxy had to do was keep out of trouble, keep out of the limelight and keep out of the newspapers...

Scene Seventeen

(We are in flashback. Enter **DIANA** *[played by actress playing* **MISS APPLEBY***].)*

DIANA. I've changed my mind. I want a divorce!

CAD. What? We've been through all this... I haven't seen Violetta once since our agreement.

DIANA. Maybe not. But our marriage is a sham, and I can't bear another minute of it. I'm leaving you.

*(***CAD*** breaks down.)*

CAD. You can't! How dare you leave me! You still love me, obviously.

DIANA. I don't. And I've met a man who deserves my love. He's honourable, decent and kind.

CAD. Who is this weedy, bedwetting drip?!

DIANA. It's Freddy Duncatton. And he's not a weed. He won the Military Cross.

CAD. *(To audience.)* Eurgh! These beastly medals again.

(To **DIANA***.)* How could you?

DIANA. Freddy and I found we had a lot in common. We both detest you.

CAD. *(Weeping.)* My wife! My best friend!

(To audience.) My marriage over...at last! With one bound our hero is free!

(To **DIANA***.)* I am prepared to accede to your demand and agree that our marriage be terminated on the grounds of your admission of adultery with Freddy Duncatton.

DIANA. I was thinking it would be terminated on the grounds of your admission of YOUR adultery with Violetta.

CAD. Have you any proof of that?

DIANA. No, but then nor do you have any proof of my affair.

CAD. Hmm. You see, that's where you're wrong. I did have an inkling that something was up, so employed the services of a private investigator who has, I'm afraid to say, some rather compromising photographs of you both in a small dreary hotel in Goring.

DIANA. You really are a complete and utter...

(She weeps and leaves.)

CAD. Victim.

(To audience.) I emerged as the poor, betrayed and deeply wronged husband with my reputation intact and I generously allowed custody of...er...Our daughter...to her mother in return for complete silence on the matter of my own understandable lapses of marital fidelity.

*(We are back in the present, with **CAD** dictating and wiping away a tear.)*

*(To **MISS APPLEBY**.)* I feel a child should stay with the mother, irrespective of the rights or wrongs of the unfortunate situation. It was hard for me, obviously, as I was heartbroken. After so much betrayal, I wondered in my solitude if I could ever trust anyone to love them again.

*(**MISS APPLEBY** looks softened.)*

(To audience.) Once again I was my own man, footloose and scandal-free, and as a lonely bachelor invited to every decent dinner in town. Boo hoo for poor old Foxy!

*(**CAD** triumphantly straightens his bow tie, smoothes down his hair and admires himself in the mirror. Back-projected headline of* Tatler *gossip column: 'MAN ABOUT TOWN – LADIES ON THE HUNT FOR FOX (INGLEBY)'.)*

(To audience.) My private life was flourishing and so I thought was my public life. Old Foxy was summoned to see the Prime Minister himself – in Downing Street!

Scene Eighteen

(**CAD** *at PM's door.*)

CAD. *(To audience.)* My first time in Number 10 – but probably not my last! Time to wheel out the legendary Fox-Ingleby charm.

(*He knocks.*)

PRIME MINISTER. Enter!

(**PRIME MINISTER** [*also played by actor playing* **MR COLLINS**, *but younger, more suave and upper class*].)

CAD. You wanted to see me Prime Minister. Does this by any chance mean promotion?

PRIME MINISTER. *(Angry.)* No it bloody well doesn't, Fox-Ingleby you fool! These war profiteering allegations against you are getting damned uncomfortable.

They reek of corruption and an unpatriotic lack of scruples.

CAD. I deny everything.

PRIME MINISTER. Of course you do. This man Hereward now says he has further proof of your wartime profiteering! He says you have shares in a munitions company.

CAD. That's a damned lie!

(To audience.) I sold the shares years ago! To my daughter! And she has wisely sold them to a banker in Switzerland. Clever girl – and she was only three at the time!

PRIME MINISTER. Listen, Fox-Ingleby, the public really don't like the idea of their elected representatives making a fortune out of the war at a time of national austerity. Are you with me?

CAD. Absolutely Prime Minister, you have my full support...

PRIME MINISTER. Well you don't have mine! And frankly, this unsavoury business could ruin you – and more importantly ME! So, if anyone is going to be thrown under the Clapham omnibus, it's you. Understood?

CAD. *(Affronted.)* I'm sorry Prime Minister, but I find these insinuations incredibly offensive. How dare anyone question my patriotism! Would the country's interests have been served if I had NOT made the brave decision to take away the contract from a dangerously pro-German armaments manufacturer?

(To audience.) In fact that story wasn't true. The rival munitions company *wasn't* actually pro-German – but it *could* have been.

(To **PRIME MINISTER***.)* Should I have risked us losing the war rather than standing up for good old Anglo-American capitalism? Is that what YOU believe, Prime Minister? It sounds suspiciously like international socialism to me!

(To audience.) Phew! If that doesn't get me off the hook, nothing will!

(Pause as **PRIME MINISTER** *looks at him.)*

PRIME MINISTER. Nice try, Fox-Ingleby. Now, either clear your name or clear your desk!

CAD. *(Deflated.)* Yes sir.

PRIME MINISTER. And by the way – I don't want to hear any more about your marital shenanigans either!

CAD. But Sir, I was the innocent party

PRIME MINISTER. Don't insult my intelligence Fox-Ingleby.

(Phone rings. **PRIME MINISTER** *answers.)*

PRIME MINISTER. Hello? Oh. A long distance call from the United States of America?

(To **CAD.***)* It's for you.

> *(***CAD*** takes receiver. We see* **VIOLETTA** *screaming at him down the phone.)*

VIOLETTA. *(Voice offstage.)* You lousy bum Fox-Ingleby!! You can't hide from me! You may have scammed your dimwit wife and got her to take the rap – but I ain't finished with you Foxy! When I divorce Winslow your name's gonna be mud!

CAD. Ha! Ha! Mother, I told you not to ring me at work! I really have to go, the Prime Minister is very busy.

> *(***PRIME MINISTER*** looks on.)*

VIOLETTA. No dice buddy boy! You can't smooth-talk your way out of this one! Prepare to get your British butt kicked into history!

> *(***CAD*** puts the phone down.)*

CAD. Thank you mother. I will certainly pass on your best wishes to the Prime Minister. And do enjoy your last-minute holiday in America.

PRIME MINISTER. You were just leaving. Probably for good.

> *(***CAD*** holds out his hand to shake.* **PRIME MINISTER** *waves him away instead.)*

CAD. *(To audience.)* It was clear that the game was up. I couldn't see a way out. My whole world was crashing down on me. I had no alternative.

Scene Nineteen

(Still in flashback. We see the podium as in the very first scene of the play. The **CAD** *appears again, as he did then, in sombre mood. Back-projected, we see once again the newspaper headline from the 1920s: 'BELEAGUERED FOX-INGLEBY MP TO MAKE STATEMENT'.)*

CAD. Ladies and Gentlemen it is with a heavy heart that I address you this afternoon. In recent weeks I have been the victim of rumours and gossip bordering on character assassination. These smears are as false as they are egregious. I acknowledge that I may have become a distraction from the very important business of government. So I have reflected on my record and examined my own conscience – and after much careful consideration I have decided to…resign with immediate effect.

(To audience.) …and then I thought, 'No! I'm not going to make that speech!' Why the change of mind? I'll tell you.

(He looks to the heavens.)

(To audience.) I thought of my proud lineage and I felt the hand of history on my shoulder. But it wasn't the hand of history – it was the beady eye of Old Granny Ingleby looking down on me fondly from the heavens… and I thought I heard her voice echoing down the ages, like an angel…

Scene Twenty

*(Suddenly **GRANNY INGLEBY** comes to life in her portrait giving **CAD** a huge fright.)*

GRANNY INGLEBY. Stop being such a weak and spineless milksop you half-baked halibut!

CAD. Granny – it's you!

(He cowers, waiting to be hit.)

GRANNY INGLEBY. You're just a jumped-up jellyfish! Don't resign! Don't be a coward!

CAD. *(Cowering.)* All right Granny, whatever you say – just please don't hit me!

(She hits him anyway from the picture.)

GRANNY INGLEBY. Shut up, boy and like I say, always, ALWAYS remember this...

*(**CAD** looks up expectantly. Dramatic pause.)*

No, it's gone again.

*(**GRANNY** fades into the picture.)*

CAD. *(To audience.)* Wise words. So I didn't resign. The ghost of Granny had shown me the way.

(There is a thunderclap, and the sound of rain.)

So damn the Prime Minister! Damn Cyril Hereward! And damn Violetta! If they think I'm going to do the decent thing, then they don't know Edward Percival Hercules Hotspur Galahad Alexander...Boadicea... Fox-Ingleby! The 320th!

(He rips up his resignation speech and exits.)

Scene Twenty-One

(We are now in the present, in real time. All the action from now is current. **MR COLLINS** *reappears. We are back in the Cad's study. He holds a bunch of flowers. Which he hastily hides when* **MISS APPLEBY** *enters with umbrella.)*

MISS APPLEBY. It's still raining.

MR COLLINS. How was your poetry evening?

MISS APPLEBY. Long. Any sign of the Political Titan?

MR COLLINS. No. The old Fox seems to have 'gone to ground.'

MISS APPLEBY. Oh very good!

MR COLLINS. Thank you. Do you think he can he possibly survive? The rumours say he's facing both a financial scandal and being named in a messy divorce.

MISS APPLEBY. Most MPs are content with one or the other.

*(***MR COLLINS*** laughs.)*

Where does that leave his memoirs?

MR COLLINS. Unfinished. Like the Symphony. Only with less harmony.

*(***MISS APPLEBY*** laughs.)*

MISS APPLEBY. So what do we do now?

MR COLLINS. I don't know Miss Appleby.

MISS APPLEBY. Constance.

MR COLLINS. Constance. What a charming name. I'm not very good at this sort of thing…but we could perhaps go for…a cup of tea?

MISS APPLEBY. You and me?

MR COLLINS. *(Embarrassed.)* Yes.

MISS APPLEBY. Are you asking me out?

MR COLLINS. Not if you…

MISS APPLEBY. You're blushing, Mr Collins! You are! How sweet.

MR COLLINS. *(Regaining confidence.)* It's Henry. We could talk about poetry, or the weather…or how beastly our employer is.

MISS APPLEBY. He's not *all* bad.

MR COLLINS. Are we talking about the same Fox-Ingleby?

(She laughs.)

And technically, he's not actually our employer as he still hasn't actually paid us anything.

(They both laugh.)

So is tea a possibility…?

(There is a slight awkwardness between them.)

*(**CAD** enters in a hurry.)*

CAD. Sorry to keep you – I just popped out to buy a paper.

MISS APPLEBY. We were wondering – are we continuing with this autobiography?

CAD. Whyever not?

MR COLLINS. It doesn't look like it will have a happy ending.

CAD. It isn't finished yet.

MR COLLINS. But with respect, it does look as though *you* might be.

CAD. You'd like that wouldn't you?

MR COLLINS. Not at all – I'm hoping to get paid!

CAD. And so you will be. We *will* finish my story. There's a last chapter yet to be written, in which our hero triumphs over the Lilliputian pygmies bent on destroying a brilliant career.

MR COLLINS. *(Unsympathetically.)* And how does he do that?

CAD. *(To audience.)* It is time for action. To put my affairs in order. Starting with the divorce proceedings of Buddington Starret versus Buddington Starret. A matter which requires a voyage to New York for an emotional meeting with Mr Violetta.

Scene Twenty-Two

(We hear ship's foghorn, seagulls, crashing waves and a miniature ocean liner steams across the stage. We then hear American jazz music, police sirens, car horns.)

(We see **WINSLOW** *[played by the actor playing* **MR COLLINS***] weeping into his martini.* **CAD** *sits with him.)*

WINSLOW. I'm losing the most important thing in my life! How could you do this to me?

CAD. I'm sorry Winslow. These things happen.

WINSLOW. I thought we were friends. But you betrayed me. And now you want to take away everything!

CAD. That's right. If you allow Violetta a divorce, you will never see my money again!

*(***WINSLOW*** breaks down.)*

WINSLOW. But I *love* your money! You don't understand. Your money completes me. Without your investment I'm nothing. I'm gonna be seriously overstretched. We've had an equity slump, which means that I've been shorting the dollar and that's left me really exposed, and if you pull out now and word gets around there will be an investor run endangering our entire leverage system...and have I told you we're under pressure on pork futures?

CAD. *(To audience.)* I'll have to buy myself four cigars. This is going to be a long, long night.

(We hear ship's foghorn, seagulls, crashing waves and the miniature ocean liner steams back again. We then hear English music hall music, Big Ben, etc.)

Scene Twenty-Three

(We are back with the **MISS APPLEBY.***)*

CAD. I'm back. Mission accomplished!

MISS APPLEBY. But what happened?

CAD. Suffice to say that Winslow came to realise a divorce citing his major investor as co-respondent would be unwise – and might end up with him seeking a new position on the window ledge of the seventeenth floor of his office on Wall Street. And so we resolved to remain faithful and true to each other as stockbroker and client.

MISS APPLEBY. How touching. And they say that romance is dead.

> *(Enter* **MR COLLINS***, breathlessly, with copy of the* Evening Sketch.*)*

MR COLLINS. The Hereward story is out!

MISS APPLEBY. What?

MR COLLINS. Front page.

> *(***MISS APPLEBY** *grabs paper. We see back-projected the newspaper headline: 'WARTIME VETERAN IN TRAGIC BREAKDOWN'.)*

MISS APPLEBY. Oh my goodness!

> *(She reads.)*

'The sad story of the discredited former officer.'

> *(***MR COLLINS** *grabs paper back.)*

MR COLLINS. But it's not about YOU – it's about Hereward.

CAD. Yes, it's about a bitter and disappointed obsessive damaged by his traumatic experience and looking for someone to blame for the failure of his life.

MR COLLINS. How do you know?

CAD. I wrote it. Well, dictated it.

MISS APPLEBY. I don't understand – why have they published it?

CAD. Because they have a brilliant new proprietor with an eye for a good story. Remember when I said I was popping out to buy a paper?

MR COLLINS. You didn't!?

CAD. It rather appears I did.

MR COLLINS. Where did you get the money?

CAD. Sadly I've had to sell the Grantly Manor Estate to a developer who has exciting plans for a splendid new gasworks on the site of the boring old beech wood.

MR COLLINS. But what of your legacy? Your family history? Your noble rural heritage?

CAD. Don't be such a snob. This is progress. Energy for the workers. This is the future. My newspaper will be supporting it wholeheartedly.

MR COLLINS. So you've finally become a baron. Even if it's only a press baron.

CAD. And a good thing too! Otherwise I wouldn't have been able to sack Hereward, and the public would have been fed a tissue of lies written by an embittered fantasist with an axe to grind.

MISS APPLEBY. What's to stop Hereward selling his story elsewhere?

CAD. You really do know nothing about how this country works, Miss Appleby! There's a code of honour amongst we newspaper proprietors. We don't publish stories about each other. It's what the Mafia call 'omerta'.

MISS APPLEBY. What?

CAD. It's an unwritten law. Certain things remain... unwritten.

MR COLLINS. Poor old Hereward...

CAD. *(To audience.)* Nonsense. The man is down, and now's the time to give him a good kicking. Though one doesn't want to appear uncharitable.

(To **MR COLLINS.***)* Of course I've done the decent thing and launched an appeal to readers to help this sad one-armed war victim in his twilight years in a home for the feeble of mind.

MR COLLINS. That's cruel.

CAD. Not as cruel as if I had headlined the appeal 'Give this fellow a hand.' But I'm better than that. And as recent events prove I *am* better than everyone!

MISS APPLEBY. You are extraordinarily arrogant!

CAD. True! One wouldn't want to be AVERAGELY arrogant!

(She laughs despite herself.)

So...I have decided to call a press conference to set matters straight and to lay out my future. Now there is much to be done. I have a speech to prepare. Probably the most important speech of my political career. Miss Appleby, I shall need your assistance. I have a proposal to put to you. Mr Collins, I shall need YOU to attend the speech and lead the applause at the correct moment. Now, to work...

*(***MR COLLINS** *and* **MISS APPLEBY** *help move the lectern from the opening scene to centre stage again.)*

Scene Twenty-Four

(**CAD** *solemnly addresses the nation once again. Back projected, we see once again the newspaper headline from the 1920s: 'BELEAGUERED FOX-INGLEBY MP TO MAKE STATEMENT'.*)

CAD. Ladies and Gentlemen it is with a heavy heart that I address you this afternoon. In recent weeks I have been the victim of rumours and gossip bordering on character assassination.

> (**MR COLLINS** *leads the applause at this inappropriate moment.* **CAD** *glowers at him.*)

These smears are as false as they are egregious. I have even been called a 'Cad'. I acknowledge that I may have become a distraction from the very important business of government. So I have reflected on my record and examined my own conscience – and after much careful consideration I have decided to…

> (*Pause.*)

…stay on as Minister of the Crown and *remain* as Member of Parliament for South East Midhamptonshire.

> (**MR COLLINS** *applauds wildly. We hear a crescendo of applause behind him and the strains of "Jerusalem" in the background.*)

I have fought off my enemies, rescued my good name and stand before you with my reputation intact. For let us not forget that I helped to win the war and helped to reconstruct the world after the war! I have made this country a land fit for heroes by devoting my life to public service – and above all I have made Britain a better place for women to live and prosper!

("Jerusalem" builds.)

If I am to be a role model for future generations, so be it. May other great men follow in my footsteps. I am proud of my achievements, and proud of the nation that allows men such as I to fulfil their destiny and perhaps to occupy the highest office in the land – though that is not for me to say.

*(Massive applause – only **MR COLLINS** is not clapping. "Jerusalem" fades.)*

I would like to thank you all for your support. I could not have survived without your kindness and loyalty. Above all, I would like to thank my wife...

*(At this point **MISS APPLEBY** shyly appears at his side with flowers.)*

My new wife, the former Miss Constance Appleby, who I am now proud to call *Mrs Edward Fox-Ingleby*!

*(They kiss as the crowd cheers wildly. **MR COLLINS** holds his head in his hands and sadly throws his bunch of flowers away.)*

(We hear Vivaldi's "Gloria" as balloons festoon the stage and confetti rains down from on high.)

End

(During bows, we see final back-projected headlines:)

READ 'THE AUTOBIOGRAPHY OF A TITAN' EXCLUSIVELY SERIALISED IN THE EVENING SKETCH

'THE BEST BOOK ABOUT ANY SUBJECT, BY ANYONE, EVER' – EVENING SKETCH

'A BOOK THAT'S RIGHT WHERE EVERY OTHER BOOK IS WRONG' – EVENING SKETCH

'AN UNSPEAKABLY FRIVOLOUS AND CYNICAL CONCOCTION THAT SHOWS THE ENGLISH PLUTOCRAT WITHOUT HIS MASK. THIS IS THE FACE OF THE PEOPLE WE MUST OVERTHROW' – JOSEF GOEBBELS, GOEBBELS DIARIES, DECEMBER 8 1940

www.ingramcontent.com/pod-product-compliance
Ingram Content Group UK Ltd.
Pitfield, Milton Keynes, MK11 3LW, UK
UKHW020905190225
455302UK00010B/483